LITTLE GIANT® ENCYCLOPEDIA

Tea Leaf Reading

LITTLE GIANT® ENCYCLOPEDIA

Tea Leaf Reading

JACKY SACH

STERLING

New York / London

www.sterlingpublishing.com

STERLING and the distinctive Sterling logo are registered trademarks
of Sterling Publishing Co., Inc.

Library of Congress Cataloging-in-Publication Data
Sach, Jacky.
Little giant encyclopedia. Tea leaf reading / Jacky Sach.
p. cm.
Includes index.
ISBN-13: 978-1-4027-5637-5
ISBN-10: 1-4027-5637-2
1. Tea. 2. Cookery (Tea) I. Title.

TX415.S224 2008
641.3'372--dc22
2007032868

2 4 6 8 10 9 7 5 3 1

Published by Sterling Publishing Co., Inc.
387 Park Avenue South, New York, NY 10016

© 2008 by Sterling Publishing Co., Inc..

Distributed in Canada by Sterling Publishing
c/o Canadian Manda Group, 165 Dufferin Street
Toronto, Ontario, Canada M6K 3H6
Distributed in the United Kingdom by GMC Distribution Services
Castle Place, 166 High Street, Lewes, East Sussex, England BN7 1XU
Distributed in Australia by Capricorn Link (Australia) Pty. Ltd.
P.O. Box 704, Windsor, NSW 2756, Australia

Printed in China
All rights reserved

Sterling ISBN-13: 978-1-4027-5637-5
ISBN-10: 1-4027-5637-2

For information about custom editions, special sales, premium and corporate
purchases, please contact Sterling Special SalesDepartment at 800-805-5489
or mail to: specialsales@sterlingpublishing.com.

CONTENTS

Introduction

Tea is in again. Tea is popping up everywhere!
We see large tea sections in coffee shops, department
stores, and entire shops devoted entirely to tea. Tea
parties are once again hot social events (we swear).
Whether it's a gathering of little girls or a group of
adults in tea party hats out for a celebratory lunch, tea
is where it's at. You'll even find men (REAL men) drinking tea in public, unabashedly enjoying a fine cup of
steeped Camellia sinensis.

You see, everyone who is anyone knows tea these
days. Even coffeehouses have large tea sections. For
example, did you know that Starbucks carries a whole
line of tea as well? It's a tea called Tazo and it's also
carried by another famous coffee house, Seattle's Best
Coffee. In fact, on the Tazo website you can even get
your tea leaves read. Or better yet, turn to Chapter
Five and learn how to read your own—or a friend's
tea leaves. Who knows? Maybe a career change is in
your future.

You are about to enter the wide, wide world of tea. From the history of tea to every type of tea imaginable, it's all here. You will leave this experience an enlightened tea master with a new appreciation for the hot beverage that has been warming hands and hearts for hundreds and hundreds of years. You'll learn all kinds of facts about tea. For example, it has been said that apart from tourism, tea is the largest industry in India. After reading this book, you can entertain your friends and family at your next tea party with the breadth of your tea wisdom. They will be so impressed.

People have been praising the virtues of tea for hundreds of years. If you are a tea lover, you will enjoy reading what others have said about tea: from politicians to novelists, spiritual leaders to coffeehouse proprietors, rock stars (yes, the Grateful Dead even wrote about tea!) to Monty Python, everyone loves tea! Read the quotations from tea lovers dispersed through this book and use them as gift tags for your tea-related present giving and hang them by your desk for your morning office tea. Or put one on the fridge to enjoy with your morning cuppa! The website for Stash tea (http://www.stashtea.com/) has a wonderful collection of quotations from the likes of T.S. Eliot to Jethro Tull. It's a fun site to check out to share your love of tea.

Where do you fall in the tea world? Are you a tea fanatic or are you just getting to know this fabulous beverage? When you hear the word tea, do you think of…

• The local Chinese restaurant and a stainless steel pot of steaming black tea?

• Your grandmother's cozy kitchen with a homemade tea cozy and a plate of sugar cookies?

• Merry old England and a plate of shortbread biscuits? Or a big basket of scones with strawberry jam and luscious Devonshire clotted cream?

• Murky Turkish tea bars?

• Your kitchen cabinet, which is filled with unopened boxes of tea you've received as gifts and have no idea what to do with? (Please see chapter three on tea parties, and how to host one.)

• A Japanese Zen tea ceremony with monks in dark robes, your mind and heart at great peace?

• Your morning life's blood, your afternoon pick-me-up, your evening's necessity, a liquid you'd rather die than live without?

• Lunch at the Russian Tea Room with your mother, after shopping at Bloomingdale's, arms loaded with heavy bags of new clothes and shoes?

• A cup of sweetened, exotic Chai tea while you are at your local spa for a massage or a pedicure?

• A cozy cup of chamomile as you prepare to go to sleep after a long and stressful day?

• An exotic Russian samovar filled with a thick and inky dark tea?

As you can see, no matter what comes to mind, you are in very good company. And if you drew a blank on tea, well, there's hope for you yet—once you finish this

book, you're sure to be brewing up a pot of pure
pleasure soon.

   The Little Giant® Encyclopedia: Tea Leaf Reading is one-
stop shopping for your tea facts. The information in
this collection comes from many different sources,
some public property, to whom we are endlessly grateful for sharing themselves with us so generously.
Without their early efforts the great interest in tea
might have never taken place. So thanks to the following: *The Book of Tea* by Okakura Kakuzo, a classic of
Eastern experience, outlining the philosophical nuances
of tea and the tea ceremony in Japanese culture; *Tea
Leaves* by Francis Leggett & Company, written in 1900
by importing and manufacturing grocers Francis
Leggett & Company; *Telling Fortunes By Tea Leaves: How
to Read Your Fate in a Teacup* by Cicely Kent, a lovely
book written in 1922 with a wealth of information on
tea leaf reading and a wonderful dictionary of tea leaf
symbols, largely reprinted here; *Tea-Cup Reading*, and

the *Art of Fortune Telling by Tea Leaves* by A Highland Seer, another instructional book on tea leaf reading with wonderful insights into this ancient craft. Thanks to these sources for their wonderful information that we so gladly share with others. A list of other sources appears at the back of this book. Here's to the wonderful world of tea!

CHAPTER ONE:

A History of Tea

Tea has most likely been enjoyed as a hot
beverage for at least 5,000 years, but the exact history
of tea is not quite clear. There have been good educated
guesses and suppositions about the first time these
lovely leaves were used for human consumption, but
no one really knows for sure. What we do know is that
tea has warmed at the hearths of homes all across the
globe for centuries. From the Far East to the far West,
from the tropical South to the frozen North, tea has
been enjoyed by and comforted the hearts of travelers,
homebodies, warriors, homemakers, mothers, fathers,
sons, and daughters for millennia. Why not join the
masses and steep a nice cup of tea while you read the
history of this revered beverage?

Once Upon a Time…

Sometime in the mid 1400s B.C.E.,
Bodhidharma, a well-known Buddhist monk, was
instructed by his teacher to go from his homeland of
India to China to spread the teachings of Zen. When

he arrived in China, Buddhism was already thriving
and many monasteries and monks existed across the
country. So Bodhidharma traveled far, eventually making his way up the mountains to Shaolin, site of the
famous Shaolin monastery. It was here in a small cave
that he sat facing a wall, meditating in the Zen tradition
for nine long years. Legend has it that he became so
frustrated with himself for falling asleep that he cut off
his eyelids and threw them to the ground, vowing
never to sleep again. On the following day, he beheld,
with amazement, springing up from the site of his discarded eyelids, two small shrubs of an unusual appearance, such as he had never before seen. Miraculously,
tea leaves had sprouted. Bodhidharma—curious and
most likely hungry—ate the leaves, and immediately
felt within him a wonderful elevation of mind. And
who doesn't like a wonderful elevation of mind? Thus
tea came into our common culture and all who enjoy it
enjoy not only the fragrant leaves and steaming brews,

but the wonderful sense of peace that has accompanied tea drinking for millennia.

True story? Well, maybe not, but it's one for the books. Perhaps you prefer to believe that tea came from Mother Earth alone, rather than from Bodhidharma's flesh. It might make drinking the lovely brew a little more enjoyable at any rate.

Although legend credits Bodhidharma with the discovery of tea, there is no real evidence that he was the first to uncover the wonders of tea drinking. At any rate, it is easy to believe that the Chinese were first in the tea fields, and that the plant was a native of both China and Japan when it was still slumbering on the slopes of India, unpicked, unsteeped, undrunk, unhonored, and unsung.

Another Chinese legend tells that tea was discovered by the Emperor Shen Nung in 2737 B.C.E.:

The emperor was a fastidious man who, in the interests of good health, only drank boiled water. One day, as he was reclining under a wild tea tree, a gentle breeze caused a few leaves to drift down from the branches. They wafted on the caressing wind before landing in Shen Nung's water. The emperor stared at the leaves in fascination while they colored his water and excited his senses. Carefully, he put his lips to his bowl to taste the fortuitous mixture. Upon drinking the surprise concoction he found it quite tasty and refreshing. He sat quietly enjoying his newfound treat. And then shared this discovery with all in the land.

As there is no written record of tea drinking until much later, it is merely conjecture as to who discovered the wonders of brewed tea, but we are certainly most grateful someone did so!

WHERE DID THE WORD TEA COME FROM?
The word tea is of Chinese origin, from early Chinese dialect words like *tu, tchai, cha* and *tay*. These words were used to describe both the brew and the leaf.

For some of the history of tea, we turn to Francis Leggett's *Tea Leaves*, written in 1900. Although the origins of tea are not quite clear, some kind of leaf was used as early as the Chow dynasty, 1122-255 B.C.E., as we learn from the *Urh-ya*, a glossary of terms used in ancient history and poetry. This work, which is classified by subjects, has been assigned to the beginning of the Chow dynasty, but belongs more properly to the era of Confucius, 551-479 B.C. While some would argue that Confucius mentioned tea when he edited *The Book of Odes*, it is widely agreed upon by scholars that a vegetable was actually referenced and there was no mention of tea.

> *"A cup of tea excels the real..."*
> —Lian Ta Yang, Chinese poet 1878-1936

Initially, however, tea was only used as a medicinal tonic (more on tea as medicine in chapter four). As demand grew, tea farms sprang up all around Asia. Soon, tea was being enjoyed as a refreshing drink and was given as gifts in dried form, as well as in cakes and liquid form. As the popularity of the beverage grew, tea paraphernalia appeared: tea scoops, teapots, tea bowls. In fact, in China and Japan, the creation of tea bowls was, and is still, high art. An elaborate and precise rule system arose around the cultivation, gathering, processing, and enjoyment of tea. It became so popular it eventually made it into print when Lu Yu compiled the first book of tea called *Cha Chang* (a tea encyclopedia) in the eighth century.

How the inestimable qualities which lie latent in the green leaf of the tea tree or bush were discovered and developed by the Chinese is one of those mysteries we shall never solve. For it is a remarkable fact that neither the green leaf of the tea plant, nor the tea leaf dried without help from us, conveys to our senses any hint of the agreeable or valuable qualities for which tea is esteemed, and which have been developed by the art of humans. A leaf of any one of the mints, or of the sassafras tree, or of the wintergreen vine, after being crushed and bruised in the hand and applied to the nose or the mouth, makes an instant impression upon the senses of taste and smell, and at once informs us of its distinctive qualities. Not so with the tea leaf: a hundred valueless plants impress those senses more vividly than the leaf which is worth them all. Infuse the green leaf of the tea plant and the prized properties of "tea" are still wanting, but in their stead, positively deleterious qualities are said to appear.

Commercial tea must be regarded as an artificial production. A certain degree of artificial heat, of manipulation, and induced chemical changes, are the agents that develop the flavor and aroma of the tea leaf. And the nature of man's treatment and manipulation determines in large measure not only the desired flavor, but the distinguishing character of the tea, its rank as a green, a

black, or an "English Breakfast Tea," all three of which
may be evolved by skillful manipulation from the same
tea bush, at the same time.

As Chinese teas became known to the inhabitants of
other parts of Asia, and to Europeans, curiosity and
commercial interests provoked others to seek information concerning the origin and treatment of different
Chinese teas. The prices obtained by the Chinese from
foreigners for teas were most exorbitant, and generated
enormous profit for the Chinese government and
Chinese merchants. Quite naturally the Chinese saw
the danger of letting the truth concerning the origin,
manufacture, and cost of their most precious commodity
pass into the possession of other people. They strove to
prevent foreigners from penetrating to their inland tea
gardens, while plying inquisitive listeners with fairy
tales that were eagerly swallowed. They said that every
different kind of tea was the product of a different
species of plant, which bore a different name, and that

the manufacture was a most intricate process depending upon secrets confined to a very few; that the leaves could safely be plucked only at certain phases of the moon, and at certain hours of the day, and that some delicate varieties of tea leaves were plucked only by young maidens, and so on. They even allowed Europeans to believe that green tea was colored by salts of copper, on copper plates, having doubtless learned that there were European merchants who would not be deterred from vending poisonous foods provided a good fat profit attended the transaction. In short, they practiced some of the dissimulation and tricks of trade to which many merchants were addicted.

How early in the history of the Chinese that people discovered and developed the inestimable qualities of the tea plant is not known. That Chinese scholar, S. Wells Williams places the date about 350 C.E. But somewhere between 500 A.D. and 700 C.E., tea had become a favorite beverage in Chinese families.

However, as we have seen, some of the written records of that ancient people push the epoch of tea drinking back as far as 2700 B.C.E. What we do know for sure is that tea in China had obtained sufficient importance in political economy in 783 or 793 C.E. to become an object of taxation by the Chinese Government.

As early as the sixth century, caravans conveyed the silks and spices and sandalwood of China by land from the Chinese Sea westward to Roman markets on the Mediterranean, a distance of nearly 6,000 miles. But we hear no mention of the introduction of tea into Europe or western Asia until a thousand years later.

Another celebrated Buddhist, Saicho (also known as Dengyo Daishai), is credited with having introduced tea into Japan from China as early as the ninth century. It is likely that he was the first to teach the Japanese the use of the herb, for it has long been a favorite beverage in the mountains there. Saicho is thought to have taken the first tea seeds to Japan for cultivation on the grounds of his monastery. According to the website Tea Time World Wide, when Saicho introduced the tea to the Emperor Saga, the emperor enjoyed it so much he decried that five provinces near the capital were to establish tea farms.

Although known in Japan for hundreds of years, tea only gradually became the national beverage as late as the fourteenth century. After the ninth century and for four centuries thereafter, tea fell into disuse, and almost oblivion, among the Japanese. The nobility, and Buddhist priests, however, continued to drink it as a luxury.

> *"If man has no tea in him, he is incapable of understanding truth and beauty."*
>
> —Japanese Proverb

During the reign of the eighty-third Emperor, 1199-1210 C.E., the cultivation of tea was permanently

established in Japan. Around 1200, the monk Eisai,
who was founder of the Rinza sect of Zen Buddhism in
Japan, also brought tea seeds from China, which he
planted on the mountains in one of the most northern
provinces. Eisai is also credited with introducing the
Chinese custom of ceremonious tea-drinking. He presented tea seeds to Mei-ki, the abbot of the monastery
of To-gano (to whom the use of tea had been recommended for its stimulating properties), and instructed
him in the mystery of its cultivation, treatment, and
preparation. Mei-ki, who laid out plantations near Uzi,
was successful as a pupil, and even now the tea grow-
ers of that neighborhood pay tribute to his memory by
annually offering at his shrine the first gathered tea
leaves of the season. After Mei-ki established the tea
plantations, tea became much more fashionable: The
monks and their contemporaries must have discovered
tea's ability to keep them awake during those long
nights of meditation!

It was around this time that tea became an art form in Japan. With the introduction of the *Chanoyu*, or tea ceremony, tea was elevated out of the everyday into the sacred. A Japanese tea ceremony is described in chapter three of this book. Its simple form is based on the concepts of respect, harmony, purity, and tranquility. Chapter three also contains more of tea's history in the Far East.

> *"Teaism is a cult founded on the adoration of the beautiful among the sordid facts of everyday existence. It inculcates purity and harmony, the mystery of mutual charity, the romanticism of the social order."*
> —Okakura Kakuzo, *The Book of Tea*

We can state with some certainty that in those early tea years, tea most likely spread from country to country by wandering Buddhist monks.

MOVING WESTWARD:
SOME ENGLISH TEA HISTORY

Eventually tea moved west and found a home on the dining tables of the Europeans, though who introduced it first is a matter of debate. Some say it first appeared in the Netherlands in 1610. Others claim that the Portuguese first introduced tea into Europe about 1557. Benjamin Disraeli offered evidence that tea was unknown in Russian Court circles as late as 1639. But Russia and Persia seem to have naturalized tea as a beverage about the same time that it became known in England. Little is said about Persian tea drinking in modern writing upon tea, but the testimony of many travelers bears witness to the national love of tea by the Persians.

Still, others concede the honor of being the first European tea drinkers to the Dutch and believe that early English supplies of tea were obtained from Dutch

sources. In 1637, the Dutch East India Company started importing it. But it was not until several decades
later that England woke up to the fascinations of the
new drink. Dr. Samuel Johnson (a great tea enthusiast)
claims that tea was first introduced into England by
Lords Arlington and Ossory, in 1666, and really made
its debut into society when the wives of these noblemen gave it its vogue. While both the English and
Dutch East India Companies showed small samples of
tea as curiosities of "barbarian" customs very early in
the seventeenth century, tea definitely wasn't used as a
beverage in England, even by the upper classes, until
well after 1650.

In an issue of the weekly
newspaper *Mercurius Politicus*
(the predecessor of the *London
Gazette*), on September 30, 1658,
this advertisement appeared:

"That excellent and by all

psyitians approved drink called the the Chineans Tcha, by other nations Tay, alias Tee, is sold at the Sultaness Head, a Cophee-house in Swwetings Rent, by the Royal Exchange, London." This appears to be the earliest record and authentic evidence of the use of tea in England.

In fact, we must credit coffee and tea with causing the creation of the London coffeehouse. Inns, where guests were expected to lodge overnight as well as eat; restaurants, in which people rested only for a single meal; beer and spirits shops, abounded in London, but the coffeehouse ushered in a new era, and actually changed the daily habits of a large majority of representative London citizens.

"Tea's proper use is to amuse the idle and relax the studious, and dilute the full meals of those who cannot use exercise, and will not use abstinence."
—Samuel Johnson

While it is asserted a Mr. Jacobs established the first coffeehouse in England, at Oxford, it was a native of Smyrna by the name of Pasqua Rosee who first opened a coffeehouse in London, in St. Michael's Alley, Cornhill, in 1652. But only hot coffee was dispensed there, during the day and in the evening.

> *"We had a kettle, we let it leak: Our not repairing made it worse. We haven't had any tea for a week...The bottom is out of the Universe."*
> —Rudyard Kipling

Coffeehouses soon increased in number and extended over the business districts of London. Businessmen quickly recognized the value of a beverage that cleared one's mental vision while refreshing and stimulating both mind and body (ah, the benefits of caffeine), and repaired to the coffeehouse at all hours for the joint purpose of drinking coffee and transacting business.

Coffeehouses became the Commercial Exchanges of London, and they were also the precursors of modern English clubs. Men of affairs, statesmen, literary celebrities, artists, naval, and military officers all retired to the coffeehouses to meet each other, to hear and discuss the serious topics and the light gossip of the day.

> *"Tea is proper both winter and summer, preserving in perfect health until extreme old age, and it maketh the body active and lusty."*
>
> —Thomas Garraway, proprietor of Garraway's Coffee house

The introduction of tea gave the coffeehouses another strong hold upon their customers, and hot chocolate as a beverage soon followed. Among the early sellers of lovely hot drinks was Thomas Garraway, the founder of Garraway's, a coffeehouse that claimed the honor of being first to offer tea in leaf and drink for public sale, in 1657. Garraway's, a four-story brick coffeehouse on Exchange Alley in London, first opened in 1659 and was a meeting place for Londoners for 216 years, before it was pulled down to make room for other structures, in 1873. Garraway left a memorial in the form of a famous tea circular. *Garway's* (it was later changed to Garraway's) *Famous Circular* is so often misquoted that we've printed the original prose here. It was originally posted in 1660.

AN EXACT DESCRIPTION OF THE GROWTH, QUALITY AND VIRTUES OF THE TEA LEAF,

BY THOMAS GARRAWAY,

In Exchange Alley, near the Royal Exchange, in London, Tobacconist, and Seller and Retailer of Tea and Coffee.

"Tea is generally brought from China, and groweth there

upon little shrubs and bushes, the branches whereof are
well garnished with white flowers, that are yellow within, of the bigness and fashion of sweet-brier, but in smell
unlike, bearing thin green leaves, about the brightness
of Scordium, Myrtle or Sumack. This plant has been
reported to grow wild only, but doth not: for they plant it
in their gardens about four foot distance and it groweth
about four foot high, and of the seeds they maintain and
increase their stock. Of all places in China this plant
groweth in greatest plenty in the province of Xemsi, lati-
tude 36 degrees bordering up on the west of the province
of Namking, near the city of day, and drying them in the
shade or in iron pans, over a gentle fire, till the humidity
be exhausted, then put close up in leaden pots, preserve
them for their drink, TEA, which is used at meals, and
upon all visits and entertainments in private families,
and in the palaces of grandees; and it is averred by a
padre of Macao, native of Japan, that the best tea ought
to be gathered but by virgins who are destined for this

work, and such, 'quae non dum manstrua patiuntur; gemmae quae nascuntur in summitate arbuscula servantur Imperatori, acpraecipuis e jus dynastus: quae autem infra nasccuntur adlatera, populo conceduntur.' *The said leaf is of such known virtues, that those very nations so famous for antiquity, knowledge and wisdom, do frequently sell it among themselves for twice its weight in silver; and the high estimation of the drink made therewith hath occasioned an enquiry into the nature threrof amongst the most intelligent persons of all nations that have travelled in those parts, who, after exact trial and experience by all ways imaginable, have commended it to the use of their several countries, and for its virtues and operations, particularly as followeth, viz: The quality is moderately hot, proper for winter and summer. The drink is declared to be most wholesome, preserving in perfect health until extreme old age. The particular virtues are these; It maketh the body active and lusty. It helpeth the headache, giddiness* and heaviness thereof. It removeth the obstructions of the spleen. It is very good against the stone and gravel, cleaning the kidneys and ureters, being drank with virgin's honey, instead of sugar. It taketh away the difficulty of breathing, opening obstructions. It is good against tipitude, distillations, and cleareth the sight. It removeth lassitude, and cleanseth and purifieth acrid humours, and a hot liver. It is good against crudities, strengthening the weakness of the ventricle, or stomach, causing good appetite and digestion, and particularly for men of corpulent body, and such as are great eaters of flesh. It vanquisheth heavy dreams, easeth the frame, and strengtheneth the memory. It overcometh superfluous sleep, and prevents sleepiness in general; a draught of the infusion being taken, so that without trouble, whole nights may be spent in study, without hurt to the body, in that it moderately healeth and bindeth the mouth of the stomach. It prevents and cures agues, surfets, and fevers, by infusing a fit quantity of the leaf, thereby provoking a most gentle vomit and breathing of the pores, and hath been given with wonderful success. It (being prepaired and drank with milk and water) strengthenth the inward parts, and prevents consumption; and powerfully assuageth the pains of the bowels, or griping of the guts, and looseness. It is good for colds, dropsys, and scurvys, if properly infused, purging the body by sweat and urine, and expelleth infection. It driveth away all pains of the collick proceeding from wind, and purgeth safely the gall. And that the virtues and excellences of this leaf and drink are many and great is evident and manifest by the high esteem and use of it (especially of late years) among the physicians and knowing men of France, Italy, Holland and in England it hath been sold in the leaf for six pounds (sterling) and sometimes for ten pounds the pound weight; and in respect of its former scarceness and dearness it hath been only used as a regalia in high treatments and entertainments, and presents made thereof to princes and grandees till the year 1657. The said *Thomas Gaeway* did purchase a quantity thereof, and first publicly sold the said tea in leaf and drink, made according to the directions of the most knowing merchants and travelers in those eastern countries; and upon knowledge and experience of the said *Garway's* continued care and industry in obtaining the best tea, and making drink thereof, very many noblemen, physicians and merchants, and gentlemen of quality, have ever since sent to him for the said leaf, and daily resort to his house in *Exchange Alley* aforesaid, to drink the tea thereof. And that ignorance nor envy may have no ground or power to report or suggest that which is here asserted, of the virtues and excellencies of this precious leaf and drink, hath more design than truth, for the justification of himself, and the satisfaction of others, he hath here enumerated several authors, who in their learned works have expressly written and asserted the same and much more in honor of this noble leaf and drink, viz—Bontius, Riccius, Jarricus, Almeyda.

Horstius, Alvarez Semeda, Martinivus in his China Atlas, and Alexander de Rhodes in his Voyage and Missions, in a large discourse of the ordering of this leaf, and the many virtues of the drink, printed in Paris, 1653, part x, chap.13. Thomas hath tea to sell from sixteen to fifty shillings in the pound. And whereas several persons using coffee have been accustomed to buy the powder thereof by the pound, or in lesser or greater quantities, which if kept for two days loseth much of its first goodness, and forasmuch as the berries after drying, may be kept, if need require, some months, therefore all persons living remote from London, and have occasion for the said powder, are advised to buy the said coffee-berries ready dried, which being in a mortar beaten, or in a mill ground to powder, as they use it, will so often be brisk, fresh, and fragrant, and in its full vigour and strength, as if new prepaired, to the great satisfaction of the drinkers thereof, as hath been experienced by many of the best sort, the said Thomas Garway hath always ready dried, to be sold at reasonable rates. All such as will have coffee in powder, or the berries undried, or chocolata, may, by the said Thomas Garway, besupplide to their content; with such further instructions and perfect directions how to use tea, coffee, and chocolata, as is or may be needful, and so as to be efficatious and operative, according to their several virtues."

One can only imagine how proud Garraway must have been to be one of the first merchants of tea in England. Now, have a cup of tea to wake yourself up again after that advertisement. And we thought today's commercials were too long!

Like all new things, when they have fastened on to the public's favor, tea was on everybody's lips and in everybody's mouth. A president of the English Court of Sessions complained tea was driving out beer, and indirectly hurting the farmer, in whose home, he omitted to say, the tea canister had begun to occupy a place of honor, despite the lessened demand for malt. Tea was praised to the heavens, and was supposed to be good for all the ills of the flesh. It would cure colds and consumption, clear the sight, remove lassitude, purify the liver, improve digestion, create appetite, strengthen the memory, and cure fever and ague.

One orator says, while never putting the patient in mind of his disease, it cheers the heart, without disordering the head; strengthens the feet of the old, and settles the heads of the young; cools the brain of the hard drinker, and warms that of the sober student; relieves the sick, and makes the healthy better. Epicures drink it for want of an appetite; bon vivants to remove the effects of a surfeit of wine; gluttons, as a remedy for indigestion; politicians, for the vertigo; doctors, for drowsiness; prudes, for the vapors; wits, for the spleen; and beaux to improve their complexions; summing up, by declaring tea to be a treat for the frugal, a regale for the luxurious, a successful agent for the man of business, and a bracer for the idle. Poets and verse-makers joined the chorus in praise of tea in Greek and Latin. One poet pictures Hebe pouring the delightful cup for the goddesses, who, finding it made their beauty brighter and their wit more brilliant, drank so deeply as to disgust Jupiter, who had forgotten that he, himself, "Drank tea that happy morn, when wise Minerva of his brain was born."

Lovers of the old and conservative customs of the table were not anxious to try the novelty, however. Others shied at it; some flirted with it in tiny teaspoonfuls; others openly defied and attacked it. Among the latter were a number of robust versifiers and physicians.

The fleshly school of doctors were only too happy to disagree with their brethren respecting the merits and demerits of the new-fangled drink; and it is hard to say which were most bitter, the friends or the foes of tea. One doctor even attributed the discovery of a number of new diseases to the debility borne of daily tea drinking. Another denied that it had either taste or fragrance, owing its reputation entirely to the peculiar vessels and water used by the Chinese, so that it was folly to partake of it, unless tea-drinkers could supply themselves with pure water and the fragrant, hygienic teapots.

In spite of the array of old-fashioned doctors, wits, and lovers of the pipe and bottle who opposed evil effects, sneered at the finely bred men of England being turned into women, and grumbled at the stingy custom of calling for dishwater after dinner, the custom of tea drinking continued to grow. By 1689 the sale of the leaf had increased sufficiently to make it politic to reduce the tax on it.

Tea grew in popular favor, both privately and publicly. The custom had now become so general that every wife looked upon the teapot, cups, and caddy to be as much her right by marriage as the wedding ring itself.

Fine ladies enjoyed the crowded public entertainments
with tea below stairs and ventilators above. Citizens,
fortunate enough to have leaden roofs to their houses,
took their tea and their ease thereon. On Sundays, finding the country in Kensington, Hampstead, Highgate,
Islington, and Stepney a much better time than church,
the people flocked to those suburban resorts with their
wives and children, to take tea under the trees.

London soon became surrounded with tea-gardens,
the most popular being Sadlier's Wells, Merlin's Cave,
Cromwell Gardens, Jenny's Whim, Cuper Gardens,
London Spa, and the White Conduit House, where
there was quite a lot of tea consumption!

It was in those early years of the nineteenth century
that tea firmly and permanently established itself in the
humbler households of England. Its economical promi-
nence elicited from William Cobbett, the economist
and editor, a declaration that from eleven to twelve
pounds of tea constituted the average annual

indulgence of a cottager's family. According to Wendy Rasmussen and Rick Rhinehart in *Tea Basics*, by 1800 nearly 24 million pounds of tea were being imported annually into England. The English have been synonymous with tea ever since.

In the early nineteenth century, the tradition of afternoon tea appeared in high society. According to Jane Pettigrew in *The Tea Companion*, we can thank the seventh Duchess of Bedford for this innovation. Anna, the Duchess, apparently felt the gap between her light luncheon and her late evening meal was just too long.

 She said she experienced a "sinking feeling" as the day wore on. In order to stave off her hunger she asked her maid to bring her in a pot of hot tea to her room with a small snack. Shortly thereafter, she started asking her friends to join her in her late afternoon break.

It wasn't long before the practice spread within her fashionable circle and ladies all over London were enjoying a late afternoon tea. Gossips, sandwiches, tea, and sweets make for wonderful diversion, and nineteenth century London took to tea with unbounded enthusiasm and excitement.

> *"Nowhere is the English genius of domesticity more notably evident that in the festival of afternoon tea. The mere chink of cups and saucers turns the mind to happy repose."*
>
> —George Gissing,
> *The Private Papers of Henry Ryecroft*

The Duchess of Bedford started a trend that seemed to spur an entire industry to growth. Soon china companies, silver makers, linen companies, and designers were all creating products for sale to complement the late afternoon tea gatherings. So, next time you find

yourself in the late afternoon with a cup of tea in one
hand, a cucumber sandwich in the other—or better yet,
a cream-filled raisin scone, say a hearty thanks to Anna
of Bedford for her hungry ways!

Take That Tea and Smoke It

Now one might not readily reconcile such a delightful daily interlude as afternoon tea with trouble of any
kind. However, if one steps out of the parlor to take a
broader look at English life at this time, it is apparent
that tea was heading for a bit of trouble abroad.

England received most of its tea for consumption
from China. And under the surface of that wonderfully
civilized tea drinking, English society stood a much
darker reality. The English were drinking record
amounts of the brewed beverage, reaching numbers
nearing five billion cups a year. In order to support
their habits, the English had become major drug
traffickers. By the 1830s, few drugs scandals in the

history of the world could rival that of nineteenth-century England.

The English needed tea. The Chinese, having no use for English exports at that time, were demanding silver in payment for the tea. The English found, however, that they did have something the Chinese might want, other than their silver. The English were growing opium in India. So they started shipping it, via the East India Company—tons and tons of barrels of it—into China in exchange for silver for tea and other Chinese goods.

But the opium was having a profound effect on the Chinese and the country was filling up with drug addicts afflicted by the effects of opium consumption. The Chinese government took action, outlawing opium in 1836, but the British traders bribed Chinese officials in order to keep the opium traffic flowing. The British continued to smuggle the drug into China until some Chinese officials took action, dumping tons of smuggled opium onto a beach in Canton. The opium was washed out to sea and the British lost their tradable goods. Great Britain, angered at the Chinese already for trade restrictions, claimed that their personal property had been attacked, and sent gunboats to attack several Chinese coastal cities. The Chinese stood no chance against the modern weapons and as the first of the Opium Wars ensued, it became apparent they would lose. In 1842, the Chinese asked for peace, and signed the Treaty of Nanjing which, among other things, ceded Hong Kong to the British.

Tea in America

Long before New York was New York, it was known as
New Amsterdam, and it was the capital of the British
colonies. It was to New Amsterdam that the Dutch
brought tea in the 1600s, starting a way of life in the
U.S. that continues to this day.

Tea took off in the Manhattan as it had in London,
following the Duchess of Bedford's lead. Coffee and tea
houses sprung up, as did purveyors of fine china, silver, and good linens. Special water pumps were even
installed on Manhattan Island to ensure a high quality
drinking water for the tea loving masses. However, it
took some time before the afternoon tea spread to the
neighboring colonies. Each developed their own preferences, some in choosing to boil the tea leaves and eat
them with salt and butter. (Not recommended.) As in
England, there were high teas (such as afternoon tea)
and low teas, where the peasants boiled their water for
tea with heartier fare. But tea was a symbol of society

and companionship: a means of sharing a cup of comfort with a neighbor and friend. Before too long, other cities followed Manhattan's social lead, with Philadelphia and Boston also hosting afternoon teas. Although Boston hosted a tea party of an entirely different kind.

> "There is a great deal of poetry and fine sentiment in a chest of tea."
>
> —Ralph Waldo Emerson

Taxation without Representation

In an effort to stabilize trade (in their favor) and rid the colonies of French influence, the English had gone to war with the French in what came to be known as the French and Indian War. As a result of the war, England had a few extra bills to foot. In an effort to pass on the expense, they passed a series of taxes that came to be known as the Townsend Act (after Charles

Townsend, who presented the first tax measure to
Parliament). Parliament felt that the colonies should
foot part of the bill for the war that had been fought to
help them out.

The colonies railed against the taxes and rebellions
ensued. Parliament reacted with more taxes and trade
restrictions, and, in June of 1767, a series of taxes
were levied.

In May of 1773, the East India Company was sitting
on tons of tea it couldn't seem to unload in England.
Parliament authorized the Company to export the tea
for sale to the colonists. To avoid the East India
Company's impending bankruptcy, Parliament allowed
them to export the tea without the usual tariffs and
duties. Now the East India Company was posed to
undercut the colonists in price and quantity on tea.
This became known as the Tea Act of 1773 and proved
to be the last straw for the colonists who rallied against
"Taxation without representation."

On November 27, 1773, three ships from the East India Company fully loaded with tea landed at Boston Harbor, but the colonists stopped them from discharging their cargo. They knew something needed to be done in order to stop the British government from overriding their wishes and delivering the tea for sale in their cities.

A group of men calling themselves The Sons of Liberty agreed upon a plan to rid the ships of the tea. On a cold night in December 1773, a band of men dressed as Mohawk Indians headed toward the Harbor and the three ships. Quietly and as quickly as possible, they boarded the ships and over the course of the next three hours they opened the chests and dumped all of the tea into Boston Harbor. More than 340 crates of tea were emptied into the sea before the men left all of the ships.

One can only imagine the excitement of such a time in history, for the Boston Tea Party was one of the sparks that ignited the American Revolution. Tea clearly played a pivotal role in the birth of the United States of America. One can only quietly wonder why, then, for so many years afterward, coffee warmed the hearts of most Americans. They had fought so hard for the right to drink the tea of their choosing! But fortunately, that time has come to pass and tea is stealthily sneaking up on Americans, soon to surely pass coffee in popularity on American shores as it has in so many other great countries.

> *"All true tea lovers not only like their tea strong, but like it a little stronger with each year that passes."*
> —George Orwell, "A Nice Cup of Tea"

QUIZ: A HISTORY OF TEA

Answers to this quiz can be found on page 460.

Before you drive down to your local tea house to have a nice cup with a friend, make sure you know the answer to these questions on the long and exciting history of tea.

1. Tea has been a hot beverage, most probably...

a. For 10,000 years

b. For 5,000 years

c. Since the Last Supper

d. Since The Boxer Rebellion

e. For 300 years

2. This Chinese emperor, interested in health and the sciences, most likely discovered brewed tea accidentally when a tea leaf floated into his cup of hot water:

a. Eisai

b. Bodhidharma

c. Shen Nung

d. Confucius

e. Mao Tse Tung

3. True or False: Tea as a brewed beverage was mostly likely spread from country to country in the early years by Trappist Monks.

4. Brewed tea originally appeared in…

a. England

b. China

c. Persia

d. Japan

e. India

5. True or False: Tea was universally greeted in England with great enthusiasm and all welcomed it into their homes and hearths.

6. _____ is largely credited with starting the British custom of afternoon tea in the early nineteenth century.

a. Lady Grey

b. Queen Victoria

c. Thomas Garraway

d. The Duchess of Bedford

e. Mary Shelly

7. True or False: The English traded one bad habit (opium) for one good habit (tea).

8. The Boston Tea Party was the Colonists' reaction to

a. Being forced to drink tea with milk and sugar.

b. A visit from the King.

c. A desire to overthrow tea drinking and replace it
   with coffee.

d. A Mohawk rebellion.

e. Taxation without representation.

CHAPTER TWO:

The ABCs of Tea

First, a Brief Collection of Tea Facts from around the World:

GIMME THE GREEN—The first tea enjoyed in the United States was actually the healthy green tea. The Dutch brought it over to New York (then New Amsterdam) in the 1600s.

THE PERFECT CUP—When making tea from loose tea it is optimal to use one teaspoon of loose tea per six ounces of water.

BANG FOR THE BUCK—Teas can be rated for caffeine content as follows (from most to least): black tea, green tea, oolong tea. Whereas a cup of coffee contains 60-120 milligrams of caffeine, a cup of black tea contains 25-110 milligrams.

CALMING TEA—The effect of caffeine in tea is felt more slowly as the polyphenols in tea slow the absorption rate down. So if you want a quick jolt, coffee is the answer.

ICE, ICE, BABY—Richard Blechynden, a tea plantation owner, attended the St. Louis World's Fair in 1904.

He was planning to give away samples of hot tea to the crowds who came to visit his booth. However, the heat made that idea a losing proposition. Ingeniously, to save his investment and make the fair worth his time and effort, he added buckets of ice into the brewed tea! The first iced tea was served on that day. Thank you, Mr. Blechynden!

SWEET—In the South, iced tea is the tea of choice. It's not just a summertime drink—it's served year-round with most meals. If you head down South and order a tea with your meal, you will most likely get a cup of sweetened ice tea, also known as Sweet Tea.

TONS! —Worldwide tea production in 2001 was 3,000 million tons!

THE WORLDWIDE CHOICE—Tea is the second most widely consumed beverage in the world—second only to water!

LINE THEM UP—It is estimated that 1.9 trillion cups of tea are consumed annually around the world.

LUCK OF THE IRISH—The Irish drink the most tea (per capita) followed by Kuwaitis, citizens of the United Kingdom, and Qatar. The United States falls far down on the list of cups of tea per person, per year. Even the Polish drink more tea than the Americans!

TEA NATION—India produces the most tea, followed by China and Sri Lanka.

THOMAS THE TEA MAN—There are many famous Thomases in the tea world: Thomas Twining (of Twinings Tea), Thomas Garraway, one of the first English coffeehouse owners, Thomas Lipton (of Lipton Tea), and Thomas Sullivan, inventor of the tea bag.

IT'S A SMALL WORLD—Forty countries around the world are known to grow tea.

ICED TEA—Tea should really be stored in airtight metal containers rather than plastic or glass. Do not refrigerate or freeze your tea. If stored correctly, tea can stay stable for six months or more.

STEEPING—Black tea needs to steep for three to five

minutes for a proper cup of tea, green tea can steep for one to three.

IN THE BAG—In 1908, Thomas Sullivan of New York accidentally invented the first tea bags. He was a tea merchant who delivered his samples wrapped in little decorative bags. He soon noticed that the restaurants he was delivering to were brewing the samples in these bags to prevent the mess of the loose tea leaves.

SEVENTY-SIX—percent of all tea produced is black tea.

GOOD THINGS COME IN SMALL PACKAGES— The smaller the tea leaf, the faster it infuses, so the steeping time is shorter for smaller-leafed teas.

DEFINE "CUPPA" —To the expert tea drinker, a proper cup of tea contains about six ounces of water, not the normal eight ounces we usually think of when we take out our coffee mugs.

MAKING DEPOSITS—Tea kettles need to be washed and dried occasionally to avoid the build up of mineral deposits, which can affect taste.

IT'S ALL ABOUT THE BAG— More than fifty percent of the tea in the United States is consumed by tea bag.

NOT THE REAL McCOY—Herbal teas are not technically tea but infusions of herbs or other plants. When we talk about tea we should be referring to black, green, oolong, and white tea.

GOING, GOING—Most of the tea sold all over the world is sold at tea auctions. Perhaps one day soon there will be an eBay-like website for tea auctions! But currently buyers and sellers attend auctions in person.

GO, TEA!!! —Tea's main competition for sales from other beverages comes from coffee and soda. Let's go, tea!

AMERICA LOVES TEA—The United States of America is the fourth top importer of tea around the world.

STUCK IN THE PAST—In the tea world, teas from Taiwan are still known as Formosa teas, and teas from Sri Lanka are still known as Ceylon teas.

> "...At last, I entered the world of tea."
>   —Yuan Mei (1716-98, Chinese poet)
>   from "Tea-Drinking"

So what, exactly, is tea?

Tea is a common hot or cold beverage made from the processed leaves of the Cameillia sinensis. The plant is an evergreen perennial that thrives in tropical cultures as well as subtropical cultures. If Cameillia sinensis sounds familiar to you, it might be because you are thinking of the plant Camiellia japonica, which is often planted in North American gardens. The Cameillia sinensis plant yields all teas but herbal teas, which are made from a wide variety of herbs and which are not technically teas.

First we'll take a look at black teas, green teas, and oolong teas. Then we'll cover the tremendous variety of herbal teas. It might surprise you to hear that black teas, green teas, and oolong teas come from the same plant; people still often believe that each type of tea comes from a different shrub. However, the differences in the teas you might find at your market are due to where the teas are grown—soil, elevation, and climate all affect how the tea will taste, how they are harvested, and how they are processed. Extreme weather conditions can affect harvests negatively, such as the damage caused by El Niño to Kenyan plantations in 1997, or the 1999 drought in northeast India that caused a nationwide drop in tea production. However, the opposite holds as well: favorable weather can yield banner crops in tea harvesting nations.

Experience has shown, however, that the tea plant possesses a wonderful power of accommodation to adverse conditions. In China and in the United States, it has been taught to put up with a comparatively sterile soil, dry mountain air, at heights in China reaching 6,000 feat above sea level, and occasional temperatures as low as 12-10 degree-Fahrenheit, in the midst of recurrent ice and snow.

Tea is indigenous to China, Tibet, and India, but it was transplanted into other countries successfully and is now grown all over the world in suitable climates. The countries producing the largest harvests of tea are India, China, Sri Lanka, Kenya, Indonesia, Turkey, Japan, South American, Bangladesh, and Russia. Green tea is most commonly grown in China and Japan, while India, Sri Lanka, and Kenya grow most of the nongreen teas. Tea used to be grown in the Southern United States, but tea plantations fell out of common practice in the nineteenth century and tea has not been widely harvested here since. Next, let's take a look at the tea plant itself.

Characteristics of the Tea Plant

As Francis Leggett reported in *Tea Leaves*, a tea shrub of
Chinese origin, growing among a host of common
American plants, displays no special characteristics that
would attract attention to itself. It resembles an orange
plant. Its developed leaves are smooth on the surface,
leathery in texture, dark green in color, with edges finely serrated from point almost to stalk. They are odor-
less, and when chewed in the mouth, have a mild and
not unpleasant astringency, but no other perceptible
flavor. A leaf of any familiar domestic plant, such as
the lilac, the plantain, or the apple has a stronger individuality to the sense of taste, than the green leaf of the
tea plant.

In form, tea leaves have been compared by writers to
leaves of the privet, the plum, the ash, and the willow,
but close observers know that not only do leaves of
these species represent different types, but that important variations in form occur in leaves of the same

species, and in leaves growing on a single tree or plant. The tea plant is subject to the same vagaries, and any description by comparison would be misleading.

> *"The best quality tea must have creases like the leathern boot of Tartar horseman, curl like the dewlap of a mighty bullock, unfold like a mist rising out of a ravine, gleam like a lake touched by a zephyr, and be wet and soft like a fine earth newly swept by rain."*
>
> —Lu Yu, quoted in
> Kakuzo Okakura's *The Book of Tea*

All varieties of the tea plant bear a pure white flower, averaging nearly 1¼ inches in diameter, and resembling a single white wild rose blossom. Their bunch of bright yellow stamens are so bushy and showy in some varieties that they've caused people to describe the flower as yellow in color, which is never the case.

In some Chinese plants, and in those of India, tea blossoms are very fragrant, and they have been used for scenting tea. In India, a perfume has been distilled from tea blossoms; a valuable oil is expressed from the very oily seeds. The long taproot of the tea plant renders it difficult to transplant.

Most farmed tea is grown on large plantations—often called gardens no matter the size—but individual families still struggle to grow enough to make a living and provide their communities with enough tea. Tea bushes are planted about four feet apart, each way, and they are pruned down to a height varying from three to six feet, to bring the topmost leaves within reach of the picker, as it is these leaves of the tea plant that are used to make tea. In fact, the finest teas use only the first two leaves and the bud. Tea thrives in tropical and subtropical climates with plenty of sun, shade, and rainfall. A remark often heard long ago from Indian planters was that "tea and malarious fevers flourish together." Elevation also plays into the way a tea tastes. Teas grown at higher elevations tend to have a stronger flavor than those grown at lower elevations.

The first crop of tea leaves may be gathered from the plant at three years from the seed, but a full crop is not expected until the plant is about six years old. In order to pick the first leaves, a tea shrub must be at least three feet tall. Traditionally, tea was always picked by hand. Today, harvesting machines sometimes do the job instead. Fine teas, however, are all still hand-picked.

> *"Tea with us became more than an idealization of the form of drinking; it is a religion of the art of life."*
>
> —Kakuzo Okakura, *The Book of Tea*

Although it is most likely back-breaking, exhausting work, it is quite romantic to picture the tea plantations of old where only workers carefully picked the best leaves off the top of the shrubs to ensure the highest quality tea. One can imagine the sunny skies, lines and lines of evergreen leaves, and women and men with baskets on their backs picking the leaves with great care. There is an old Chinese ballad of some thirty stanzas, which pictures the reflections of a Chinese maiden who is employed in picking tea in early spring. Here is a sampling from this old-time ballad:

"Our household dwells amidst ten thousand hills, Where the tea, north and south of the village, abundantly grows; From Chinshe to Kuhyu, unceasingly hurried, Every morning I must early rise to do my task of tea.

By earliest dawn, I at my toilet, only half dress my hair, And seizing my basket, pass the door, while yet the mist is thick; The little maids and graver dames hand in hand winding along, Ask me, 'which steep of Sunglo do you climb to-day?'

My splint-basket slung on my arm, my hair adorned with flowers, I go to the side of the Sunglo hills, and pick the

mountain tea. Amid the pathway going, we sisters one
another rally, And laughing, I point to younder village—
'there's our house!'

This pool has limpid water, and there deep the lotus grows;
Its little leaves are round as coins, and only yet half blown;
Going to the jutting verge, near a clear and shallow spot, I
try my present looks, mark how of late my face appears.

The rain is passed, the utmost leaflets show their greenish
veins; Pull down a branch, and the fragrant scent is diffused
around.

Both high and low, the yellow golden threads are now quite
culled; And my clothes and frock are dyed with odors
through and through.

The sweet and fragrant perfumes like that from the Aglaia;
In goodness and appearance my tea'll be the best in Wuyen,

*When all are picked, the new buds by next term will again
burst forth, And this morning, the last third gathered is
quite done.*

*Each picking is with toilsome labor, but yet I shun it not, My
maiden curls are all askew, my pearly fingers all be numbed;
But I only wish our tea to be of a superfine kind, To have it
equal their 'dragon's pellet,' and his 'sparrow's tongue.'*

*For a whole month, where can I catch a single leisure day?
For at earliest dawn I go to pick, and not till dusk return;
Then the deep midnight sees me still before the firing pan—
Will not labor like this my pearly complexion deface?*

*But if my face is thin, my mind is firmly fixed. So to fire my
golden buds that they shall excel all beside, But how know I,
who'll put them in jeweled cup? Whose taper fingers will
leisurely give them to the maid to draw?"*

Today, to ensure the quality of finer teas, handpicking is still the harvesting method of choice. It is only by hand that an experienced leaf picker can identify and isolate the quality leaves. As it is only at most the first few leaves and bud of each tea leaf that make up the finest teas, a mechanical harvester cannot guarantee this kind of finesse. A machine will pick a bunch of leaves off the top, often coming away with a branch as well, and this difference will be the telling between a fine, rich and strong tea and a harsher, heavier flavor.

Classes of Tea

You might be surprised to learn that there are nearly 3,000 varieties of tea to be found from around the world. However, tea may conveniently be divided into the three largest classes:

- Green Teas
- Oolong Teas
- Black Teas

We will discuss white tea as well here. All of the teas have to go through a manufacturing process before they arrive, packaged and pretty, on our kitchen shelves. Unlike Shen Nong, we do not brew fresh-picked tea leaves. First, they are prepared for us in the following ways.

Green Tea

In making green tea, the object is to expel the watery juices of the leaf and to cure or dry it with the least delay. Hence, the leaves are not exposed to the sun, but are often first dried in the air for a short time (though frequently this step is skipped). They are next exposed to heat (usually by frying over heat or steaming), which renders them flaccid and pliable (and prevents fermentation/oxidation, a process reserved for black teas and

oolongs), preparing them for the third operation of rolling, which twists the yielding leaf as seen in manufactured tea, rolls it up into balls, and squeezes out a considerable portion of its watery juices. The balls are then broken apart, and the scattered leaves are submitted to the final drying process by fire, which finishes green tea. As green tea is not oxidized, it retains its lovely green color.

Tea can be rolled by hand, by a mechanical roller (called the orthodox method) or more commonly by CTC (cut/tear/curl). The CTC machines shred and tear the tea leaves into small fragments. The smallest fragments are used for tea bag teas while the larger leaf fragments are used for loose leaf teas.

> *"Wouldn't it be dreadful to live in a country where they didn't have tea?"*
>
> —Noel Coward

Oolongs

Oolongs are delicate teas, having properties further developed than those of green teas. You could say that Oolong teas fall somewhere in the middle of green teas and black teas, as in green teas no fermentation takes place, and in black teas full fermentation occurs.

In making an Oolong tea, the leaves are first exposed to air and sun for a considerable time. An incipient fermentation takes places, which is why oolong teas are referred to as "semi-fermented" teas. There is certainly a chemical change beyond the brief preliminary drying of green tea. During this period the leaves are stirred and tossed by hand. The effect, if not the object, is to expose greater surfaces to the air, and to increase oxidation. This process is repeated several times and the leaves first begin to manifest a fragrant tea odor that the green leaf did not possess. This prolonged exposure to the air is termed "withering," and the leaves become soft and flaccid, as they do in the first artificial heating for green tea. In withering, the leaves lose about one third of their weight in moisture. The leaves are slightly bruised before the termination of this treatment, but not too much or unwanted chemical changes will begin. The fermentation (oxidation) period for oolongs is not quite as long as it is for black teas (hence "semi-fermented"). Green oolongs go through a shorter oxidation period than do Formosa oolongs, so the oxidation period is another factor in deciding the flavor of tea. Once the desired oxidation level has been reached, the leaves are exposed to high heat (usually by pan frying) to arrest the oxidation process. This exposure to higher heat removes much of the moisture from oolong teas, giving them a longer shelf life than green tea. The abbreviated oxidation process for oolong teas gives them their distinctive coppery/reddish leaf color and delicate flavor.

Black Tea

For black teas the process is much the same as for
oolongs, except the oxidation process is simply carried
further. First the plucked leaves are withered, removing
the excess moisture so they can be rolled. They are
then rolled by one of the aforementioned methods, and
allowed to oxidize fully. Experienced workers monitor
the leaves to ensure that oxidation is not allowed to
continue too long. The oxidation process changes the
chemical structure, which brings out the stronger flavor
of black teas. Once the leaves are judged to be sufficiently oxidized, they are fired in hot pans or roasted
over a high heat. This process turns the leaves black
and they lose virtually all of their moisture.

Each goes through a similar process. However, most
green teas are not allowed to oxidize, while both
oolong and black teas are oxidized to varying degrees.
Rolling hand versus using CTC methods can determine
the type and grade of tea. Finer teas are rolled by hand.

White Teas

The U.S. Tea Association has pushed internationally to give white tea a definition so that there is a standard in the industry. White tea refers to the method by which the tea is produced. According to the U.S. Tea Association, it is produced from the fresh unfurled buds of the Camellia sinensis shrub and the processing involves no withering, fermentation or rolling (it is steamed and dried). The brewed tea should be clear to pale yellow in color.

Types of Green Tea

Here is a short selection of green teas to choose from along with a note on when you might enjoy them. Once you start exploring the world of green teas, you will probably want to try even more varieties:

Bancha: Japan, a weaker, everyday tea, good for the evening.

Baozhong: Japan, often used to make Jasmine tea.

Dragon Well (Lonjing): China, one of the best teas in China, an early season tea, for special occasions.

Formosa Gunpowder: Taiwan, a good everyday tea, very refreshing.

Formosa Grand Pouchong: Taiwan, lightly fermented, good everyday tea.

Genmaicha: Japan, usually what you'll find in Japanese restaurants, basically sencha with fire-roasted rice, a good everyday tea.

Gu Zhang Mao Jian: China, slightly oxidized green tea.

Gunpowder: China, Taiwan, also called Pearl tea, good tea with strong flavor. Makes a nice iced tea.

Gyokuro: Japan, also known as Pearl Dew, very fine tea, sweet, for special occasions or special visitors.

Hojicha: Japan, a Bancha tea that is low in caffeine, good for evening.

Hyson: China and India, also called Young Hyson, everyday tea.

Matcha: Japan, ceremonial tea of Japan, powdered.

Pi Lo Chun: China, processed completely by hand, grown alongside peach, plum, and apricot trees that lend their fragrances to the leaves, for very special occasions.

Sencha: Japan, 70 percent of the country's export of green tea, a great everyday tea.

You can also get flavored green teas at your local supermarkets, specialty tea stores, or online vendors. Look for such blends as (we are not making these up!): Green Chai, Goji Berry Pomegranate Green Tea, Green Earl Grey, Green Lemon, Green Mango, Green Orange, Honey Lemon Ginseng Green, Green Peach, Green Vanilla, Green Paradise, Japanese Cherry, Moroccan Mint, Honey Chamomile Green, Green Tea with Jasmine, Pineapple and Papaya…the list goes on.

Black Teas

Here is a short selection of black teas to investigate along with a note on when you might enjoy them. You might be surprised to find such a variety of black teas as well!

Assam: from northeastern India, distinctive flecked brown and gold leaves known as "orange" when dried. A fine tea with a robust flavor. The basic tea to have on hand at all times. Best in the morning for a nice wake-up tea.

Ceylon: from Sri Lanka, where Lipton first harvested teas, a good everyday tea, ideal for iced tea.

Darjeeling: foothills of the Himalayas, reddish gold color, wonderful aroma, good at any time, but also for special occasions. Also called the champagne of teas. True Darjeeling is expensive and hard to find, so don't be fooled by blended versions you might run across.

Keemun: China, called the burgundy of teas due to the red color it produces when brewed. Smoky aroma,

sweet taste, very popular in China, makes a nice breakfast drink.

Nilgiri: India, nice tea with slight lemon flavor, usually
blended but on the rise as a stand-alone tea.

Pu'erh: China, earthy flavor, very strong, not for everyone.

Sikkim: India, near Darjeeling. Less expensive, nice
flavor, good in the afternoon, but might be hard to find
as well.

Yunnan: China, vaguely spicy "pepper" flavor, good
for iced tea.

Recommended black tea blends include: Irish
Breakfast, English Breakfast, Earl Grey, Lady Grey,
Cinnamon Spice, Plum Spice, Snappy Ginger Spice,
Raspberry, Caramel, Almond, Russian Caravan, Lapsang
Souchong, Chai.

Oolong Teas

Formosa Oolong: Taiwan, great variety within Formosa
oolongs, from everyday teas to high-grade teas.

Aromatic, good for special occasions, afternoon teas.
Pouchong: Taiwan, usually used for jasmine tea.
Excellent tea.
Ti Kuan Yin: China, highly regarded Chinese oolong,
fruity flavor.

Herbal Teas

Now, on to herbal teas, which technically aren't teas at
all, as teas are really only beverages made from the
leaves of the Cameillia sinensis plant. Brews made from
herbs are known as infusions. But who doesn't enjoy a
chamomile, peppermint or cinnamon infusion once in
a while?

You can make herbal teas by adding herbs to black,
green, and oolong teas, or you can make them from the
herbs themselves. Or you can get in the car and drive
down to the store and buy a readymade tea anytime
you like. If you'd like to make your own, here's how to
go about it. Use any of the following herbs, either from

your garden, from a local farm, or dried from your
organic market:

Angelica	Ginger	Orange Peel
Anise	Ginseng	Pau D'arco
Basil	Hawthorn Berry	Peppermint
Beebalm	Lavender	Rosemary
Black currant	Lemon Balm	Spearmint
Clove	Lemon Verbena	Thyme
Dill	Lemongrass	Valerian
Echinacea	Licorice	Vanilla
		Yerba mate

Pick the herbs of your choice, and, if fresh, wash them carefully in clean, cold water. Boil cold water and pour it over the herbs in a container safe for boiling water. Let the herbs steep for at least five minutes. Strain the liquid into a cup or teapot and voila! Instant herbal tea. You can add your own sweetener, such as sugar or honey, or drink it as is. Experiment with different herbs and fruits, and different sweeteners. Try different amounts of your herbs to see what tastes the best. A good rule of thumb is to use two tablespoons of fresh herbs per cup of tea, and one tablespoon of dried herbs. If this doesn't taste strong enough for you, add another tablespoon for the pot on your next batch. Mix and match to your heart's delight. Also, check out different websites for making herbal teas, including iced teas. A Google search will turn up a lot of resources for you!

You can also make sun-brewed tea by leaving a container of herbs and water on your porch while the sun shines. This makes a lovely iced tea made the old-fashioned way!

> *"Peter was not very well during the evening. His mother put him to bed and made some chamomile tea—and she gave a dose of it to Peter! 'One tablespoonful to be taken at bedtime.'"*
>
> —From Beatrix Potter's, *A Tale of Peter Rabbit*

Equipment

One of the wonderful things about tea is tea paraphernalia. From teapots to tea cozies, infusers to whisks, strainers to storage, developing a tea habit usually means a shopping trip is in your future.

Of course, you don't need much to have a perfect up of tea. But the choices and the selections for your tea cupboard are quite tempting.

Kettles

There are all different kinds of tea kettles to be found on the market. You can buy electric kettles, cast iron kettles, small kettles, large kettles, kettles shaped like cows, cats, pigs, and chickens. You can buy kettles in copper, ceramic, glass, iron, enamel, stainless steel, and plastic (for electric kettles). You can also just boil your water in a big pot on the stove and transfer it to your teapot or cup when you are ready. A kettle is largely a matter of personal preference. You may prefer an electric kettle for ease and to save time, but you also might prefer the old-fashioned joy of hearing a whistling kettle sound off in your kitchen. No matter what you choose, just be sure to keep it clean as mineral deposits can leave residue that will build up after time. You can clean it out with dishwashing detergent and a metal brush or scrubber. Make sure you give the kettle a good cleaning every few months.

Teapots

No one is completely sure where the teapot came from.
Some have claimed it was a Chinese invention, while
others claim Islamic influence. There is little doubt,
however, that the modern teapot is based on the
European designs of the seventeenth century. By the
eighteenth century, teapots in England were being made
out of porcelain, stoneware, and bone china, and names
such as Wedgwood and Spode appeared. Today you can
find a teapot in nearly any shape and size. There are tiny
one-person teapots and large multiple-cup teapots. Some
come with infusers built in, while others have none. You
can find teapots in any form you can possibly imagine.
There are animal-shaped teapots, teapots shaped like
chairs, teapots shaped like carriages, squat ones, tall
ones, narrow ones, fat ones. There are teapots decorated
with figures from *Alice in Wonderland*, and memorial
teapots from different times in history. There are patriotic
teapots and whimsical ones. Any color you can possibly

imagine will show up on a teapot. Your
only limit is the time you are willing to
put into a search for an ideal one.
Collecting teapots can be fun as well:
Whether it's fine china or an inexpensive
ceramic, you can have a teapot for every mood.

My mother has a collection of small teapots, called
one-person teapots, and she has tea parties for all her
friends. Each guest gets their very own pot of tea with
the tea of her choice. Teapots range in price from just a
few dollars to unimaginably expensive pieces of art.
According to the website EasternTea.com, a very rare
pair of "famille rose" coral-ground teapots and covers
from the Qianlong period
(China, 1736-1795) sold for 1.2
million dollars to a private collector in Hong Kong. You might
not want to go that high, but
you can certainly spend your

paycheck on a teapot if that's your heart's desire.

Some teapots come with a built-in infuser. Simply fill the infuser with the proper amount of tea for your needs. Pour boiling water over tea leaves in the infuser. Let steep for the proper amount of time and pull out the infuser when you are ready. If you leave the infuser in, the tea might become quite bitter, so make sure you take it out for an optimal brewing experience. You can also use a teapot that works much like French press for coffee (these are actually called tea presses) to make a good cup of tea. Simply fill the pot with the desired amount of tea and let it steep. When you are ready, push down the plunger. The plunger traps the tea leaves at the bottom of the pot so they can't escape into the brew and disturb your experience. If your teapot does not have its own infuser, you can use any of a number of infusers available on the market.

Silver Tea Sets

Some sources report that it was Queen Victoria who
first served tea on a silver tea service set. Silver tea
services first appeared in England in the early 1730s.
According to MarvelCreations.com, Paul Revere ("The
British Are Coming!") is shown in his favorite portrait
with a silver tea pot. He was a well-known, respected
silversmith himself and made many such silver sets.

I have a silver tea service handed down to me
from my English grandmother. Silver is time-consum-
ing to care for. It needs to be polished to look presenta-
ble. However, if you have time and the inclination, it's a
wonderful addition to a tea party or a more formal

dinner party. A silver tea set traditionally included a silver tray (for carrying and holding the tea necessities), sugar bowl, cream jug, slop water bowl, tea strainer and, of course, a teapot. All were, naturally, made out of silver. The slop water bowl was used either to pour old, unused cold tea from your cup before pouring a fresh one, or to drain the water used to warm the teapot, which brings us to the wonderful tip for tea.

TIP FOR A NICE, HOT POT OF TEA: If you plan to serve your tea in a teapot, warm the pot before pouring the water for tea into it. Simply pour some boiling water into the pot and slosh the water around the sides of the pot. Discard the water. This will warm it nicely and keep the tea hotter for a longer period of time. If you do this before you serve the tea to guest, you can forgo a slop bowl.

Infusers and Strainers

There are a number of different infusers you can choose from, depending on your preferences. You can use a tea ball, which is a round metal container with holes in it. The tea ball unscrews down the middle; you can add the tea and screw the two halves back together so no tea escapes. Place the tea ball into your teapot and let the water steep into the ball. After the desired steeping strength is reached, simply remove the ball. Most balls come complete with a metal "string" attached for easy grasping.

Another similar option is a mesh tea ball. There are also spring-handled infusers, which are like mesh tea-balls with a handle attached and a spring lever on the teaball itself. You can control the opening and closing of the ball by manipulating the handle. There are also spoon infusers, which are self-explanatory, and reusable tea bags. There are many different infusers to choose from, including bamboo infusers and those in the shape of an egg. Strainers also come in all different shapes and sizes, but stainless or silver are recommended. You can also use permanent filters such as the ones they now sell for coffeepots, or you can use a cotton tea net, which looks much like a fishing net but fits directly into your mug or teapot and fills with your favorite loose leaf tea. Dunk up and down and remove when the desired steeping strength is reached. And if that's not enough for you, some tea mugs come with their own infusers built in. Overwhelmed? Don't be! It's a wonderful discovery process finding out what works best for you and what will give you the optimal tea experience.

Tea Cozies

What the heck is a tea cozy, you might ask, and why do I need one?

Tea cozies are back in fashion. Beautiful designs are showing up in all kinds of tea stores. I received tea cozies for Christmas from both my mother and my mother-in-law, and they were my favorite ones yet: Homemade! Tea cozies insulate your pot, keeping your tea nice and warm while you enjoy your first cup of tea. Tea cozies come in all different fabrics from cottons to hand-knit designs. They can fit over the teapot like a dome or come up under the teapot to bunch at the top: a posy-type design. Some cozies leave holes for the spout and handle, while others cover the whole kit and kaboodle. My mother made me a hat out of a tea cozy pattern and I wore it all winter. They're versatile! Alas, if your budget

is tight and you can't manage a tea cozy, do not worry. A tea towel thrown over your pot works just as well. But treat yourself to a tea cozy one of these days: You won't regret it.

> *"Never trust a man how, when left alone in a room with a tea cozy, doesn't try it on."*
>
> —Billy Connolly

Tea Wallets

You can even buy hand-sewn tea holders to pack into your purse. Much like passport holders hold your travel documents, tea wallets hold a variety of tea bags so you are never caught without one. And, of course, you can buy tea boxes for storage of tea bags at home as well. My friend Helen has a lovely mahogany box with slots for sixteen different kinds of tea bags. It's tea heaven!

Tea Bowls and Tea Cups

Like teapots, there are a seeming infinite variety of tea
cups. Tea cups were originally tea bowls in China and you
can still find them today in Chinese and Japanese restaurants, in homes, and with collectors. Creating tea bowls is
still considered a high art. The beautiful forms and glazes
are pleasing to the eye and the touch. The Japanese tea
ceremony captures the serene beauty of the Japanese
design. The tea bowl used for this ceremony presents a
singular beauty, purity, dignity, and humility, and embod-
ies the spirit of the ceremony itself. Many masters of the
tea bowl still create bowls around the world and it's possible to catch an exhibit occasion-
ally. For more on Japanese tea
ceremonies, see chapter three.

Handles on tea vessels were
eventually added by Europeans,
as a matter of function. Tea
cups are a matter of personal

preference, of course, and you can go with fine china or a simple mug. There are also Chinese covered mugs, which have been in use since the fourteenth century.

> "You can never get a cup of tea large enough or a book long enough to suit me."
>
> —C. S. Lewis

Caddy and Caddy Spoon

Along with the introduction of tea into England in the seventeenth century came the tea caddy. A tea caddy is a container in which tea is stored. The word caddy is thought to derive from the Malay word *kati*, which is a unit of measure approximately equal to 1.33 pounds. So tea caddies were made to hold and store tea. Early tea caddies were mostly made of porcelain, glass, silver, enamel, and straw-covered metal. The earlier versions were jar-shaped, as opposed to the later box shapes that became fashionable. Most caddies were made of wood and became very popular in homes as a design element in the late eighteenth century. Many caddies are beautiful works of art and come in a variety of materials from china to mahogany to papier-mâché.

Some have single compartments, some have double, and others are divided in to three sections. In a three section caddy, you might store green tea, black tea, and sugar, but obviously you can mix it up with anything of your choosing. You can check out different styles of tea caddies online. Log onto eBay and search for Tea Caddy. You'll love what you see!

Tea Storage

You can, of course, store your tea in a tea caddy. But proper storage for tea is very important. All tea can only remain fresh for so long; you want to retain as much freshness as possible for as long as you can. Tea can become less enjoyable through prolonged exposure to light, air, odors (such a food odors), and moisture.

You don't want your tea to start tasting like onions so getting it out of the fridge or away from the food storage cabinet is always a good idea. Store tea in a cool and dry place, in an airtight container that won't allow in direct light. Metal containers are best. Most tea purveyors do not recommend that you store tea in the refrigerator or freezer.

The Perfect Cup of Tea

Ah, the quest for the ultimate cup of tea. What a pleasure it is in life to sit back with a perfectly brewed cup of tea. How you have your tea is obviously a matter of personal preference. You might prefer a cup of black tea with milk and sugar, and a cup of green tea unadorned. You might prefer black tea with honey, or a squeeze of lemon. Many people prefer their tea with nothing added. I personally enjoy black tea with a touch of organic milk, no sugar, and I prefer my green tea straight up. But regardless of whether or not you add anything to your tea, getting that perfect cup of brewed liquid comes first.

It is recommended that you make your tea with filtered or bottled spring water. Water can make or break a good cup of tea, as anyone can tell you who has ordered a cup of tea in a diner and received a really awful cup of tea made with strongly flavored local water.

For a wonderful cup of black tea or oolong tea:
- Boil your filtered or bottled spring water.
- When the water has come to a boil (but without boiling for very long), pour the tea into the teapot or tea cup to warm the vessel. Slosh the tea around the pot or cup and discard the water.
- Measure one teaspoon per six ounces of water of loose leaf tea into your infuser, teaball, teapot, etc.
- Let the tea steep for three to five minutes. Cover your pot or cup to preserve the temperature. If the tea leaf is quite small, the steeping time will be shorter. If the

tea leaf is larger, let it steep for a longer period of time. Initially, before you are familiar with a particular type of tea, you can test the tea and note how long you let it steep so you are prepared for the next cup. Do not let your tea steep too long. As soon the steeping time is up, remove the infuser or strainer from the tea and put aside. Cheers!

For a wonderful cup of green tea:

- Bring your filtered or bottled spring water to a near boil, but not a full boil as green tea is little more delicate than the black and oolong varieties.
- When the water is ready, pour the tea into the teapot or tea cup to warm the vessel. Slosh the tea around the pot or cup and discard the water.
- Again, measure one teaspoon per six ounces of water of loose leaf tea into your infuser, teaball, teapot, etc.
- Let the tea steep for one to three minutes, as green tea is more delicate and doesn't take quite as long to infuse. Cheers!

If you are making herbal tea, you can let the tea infuse for a much longer time than either black tea or green tea. Experiment until you find the infusing times that work best for you.

In *Tea Leaves*, by Francis Leggett & Company, the author gives the following advice on making the perfect tea in 1900:

HOW SHALL WE MAKE TEA?

How shall tea be drawn or infused? Is there but one standard method for all teas, or all persons? Certainly not. A method that will suit very many delicate tastes may be briefly stated: Use water as free as possible from impurities, from earthly matters like lime. If water is boiled too long its contained air is expelled and the tea will have a "flat" taste. Use an earthen teapot by preference; one that is never applied to any other purpose. A preliminary warming of the dry teapot is advised. Drop in your tea leaves, and pour on the whole quantity of water required, while at boiling temperature. Set in warm but not very hot situation to steep, avoiding so far as practicable, loss of vapor and aroma from the teapot.

Now, as to the length of time tea should steep: it will vary with different teas and different tastes. Some steep tea but three minutes; others double the time; while still others extend the time to 15 minutes. In any event, as soon as the characteristic flavor is extracted from the leaves, known by the loss of an agreeable tea-odor in the withdrawn leaves, the beverage will be improved rather than impaired by pouring it off into a clean teapot, in which the tea may then be preserved for a long time without injury.

To some tastes, a little of the tannin is agreeable, and its absence would be missed. Then as to sugar and milk: it is evidence of exaggerated personality (conceit, some call it), to declare that milk or cream or sugar injure the flavor of tea. As well insist upon a special spice being used for all viands of food because the critic likes it. As milk or cream neutralize the tannin to a considerable extent, they are so far desirable, without regard to taste.

Turn the page for a lovely poem to enjoy while you drink your perfect cup of tea:

OVER MY TEA CUP

by Charles J. Everett

This homely can of painted tin
Is casket precious in my eyes;
Its withered fragrant leaves within,
Beyond all costly gems I prize.
For those crumpled leaves of tea,
The sunbeams of long summer days,
The song of bird, the hum of bee,
The cricket's evening hymn of praise,
The gorgeous colors of sunrise,
The joy that greets each new-born day;
The glowing tints of sunset's skies,
The calm that comes with evening grey;
The chatter of contented toil,
The merry laugh of childish glee,
The tonic virtues of the soil,

Were caught and gathered with the tea.
Lifeless those withered leaves may seem,
Locked fast in slumber deep as death,
But soon the Kettle's boiling steam
May rouse to life their fragrant breath.
With sigh of deep content we breathe
The sweet mists rising lazily,
With eager, parted lips receive taste of tea.
Forlight and warmth and mood of men,
Whate'er the plant hath heard or seen
Or felt, while fixed in field or fen,
And stored within its depths serene,
Are now transmuted into thrills
Of sense or feeling, echoes faint
From peaceful perfumed tea-cladhills,
From placid Orientals quaint.
And fancies born in other lands,
Which dormant lie in magic tea,
Dream-castles fair not made with hands,

By some mysterious alchemy
Emerge from cloudland into sight,
Transform the sombre working-world,
The gloomy hours of day or night
From leaden hue to tint of gold,
Bring rest to wearied heart and brain,
Kind nature's soul to us reveal,
Enlarge the realm of Fancy's reign,
Renew the power to see and feel
The radiance of the rising sun,
The sunset's glow, the moon's pale light,
The promise of a day begun,
The rest from toil that comes with night.
And as I sip my cup of tea,
Though not a friend may be in sight,
I know that a brave company
Is taking tea with me this night.

TEA QUESTIONS

Where can I buy some Orange Pekoe?

Well, aren't you in for a big surprise. Orange Pekoe (peck-oh) is not actually a type of tea. Orange Pekoe is a term used to describe a grade of tea in the tea-grading system for black teas. Somewhere along the way, someone got confused and started to call black teas in the west, Orange Pekoes. Some examples of grading terminology include: OP (Orange Pekoe, black tea that includes the long, pointed leaves but not usually tips), FOP (for Flowery Orange Pekoe, black tea made from the end bud and first leaf), and STGFOP (Special Finest Tippy Golden Flowery Orange Pekoe. Yes, you guessed it: best of the FOP). Perhaps better known (among tea snobs) as Seems Far Too Good for Ordinary People.

No one is quite sure where the Orange in Orange Pekoe came from. It certainly has nothing to do with flavor. So stop asking the tea man for Orange Pekoe.

What kind of tea has the most caffeine?

According to the Fragrant Leaf website,
(www.FragrantLeaf.com), a Department of Nutritional
Services report provides the following ranges of caffeine
content for a cup of tea made with loose leaves:

• Black Tea: 23 - 110 mg
• Oolong Tea: 12 - 55 mg
• Green Tea: 8 - 36 mg
• White Tea: 6 - 25 mg

So black tea has the most caffeine and white tea has
the least. Of course, decaffeinated teas are found among
all the varieties of tea. And herbal "teas" have no caffeine.

What is a tea-taster?

Believe it or not, tea tasters are still used in the tea
trade both on the manufacturing side and the sales
side. Tea brokers use tea tasters to assess the value of
tea for sale. Tea tasters are also used to decide which
teas are appropriate for blends and what to add to

blends. Picture a wine taster and you're on the right track. The process is pretty much the same. In case you think this sounds strange, you might be interested to know that in 1897 Congress passed the Imported Tea Act, which created the Board of Tea Experts, headed by the office of the Federal Tea-Taster. It was the Federal Tea-Taster's job to check out the incoming clipper ships and make sure the imported tea was up to snuff. But, hold on, you won't believe this: When President Bill Clinton decreed that "The era of big government is over," in his 1996 State of the Union Address, he wasn't kidding. Among the jobs he considered fit for cuts was that of the Federal Tea-Taster's. The poor tea-taster. He was making good money: At the time of the cut, $120,000 a year was being spent on federal tea-tasting.

What is a tea brick?

Chinese tea merchants formed tea into cakes—or tea bricks—in Ancient China and continue to do so to this day, though not quite as commonly. Finely ground tea leaves were molded and pressed into brick form and used for brewing, eating, and even as money. Decorative tea bricks make unusual gifts and interesting conversation pieces. I found some at a specialty tea store in New York, but they are available online for viewing and purchase. However, I wouldn't recommend eating them.

Are tea bags inferior to loose leaf tea?

I'm sure it's an easy answer to say that loose leaf tea is far superior, but it really does depend on the brand and type of tea. Some bagged teas are excellent. And obviously tea bags have some conveniences that loose tea just doesn't offer. If you're on the go, a tea bag is a wonderful innovation. However, don't think you have to sacrifice quality. Stay away from the generic supermarket brands of tea bags and you should be fine. But I don't have to tell you that. Once you investigate some

superior teas, you'll be ruined for the rest.

It may be of note, however, that the tea that makes it into tea bags are the smallest parts of the tea leaves that are left over after the manufacturing process. These are called fannings. Tea is made up of chemicals and essential oils that give it its flavor and aroma. The more the leaves are broken up, the more the chance the oils and chemicals will dissipate, leaving the rest with an inferior taste.

> *"Women are like tea bags. They don't know how strong they are until they get into hot water."*
> —Attributed to both Nancy Reagan
> and Eleanor Roosevelt

Where did the word china come from?

According to Jane Pettigrew in her excellent book on tea, *The Tea Companion*, the word china first appeared in relation to tea equipment when the first tea wares arrived in Europe from China in the mid-seventeenth century. China came to denote all the dishes needed to serve tea.

In Good Company

In the book *Tea Leaves*, we can find the following list of others who loved tea:

- The only stimulant that Hazlitt indulged in was strong Black tea, using the very best obtainable.
- Wordsworth was a lover of tea, and he sweetened his tea beyond the taste of ordinary mortals.
- Shelly also was a lover of tea.
- Kant drank tea habitually for breakfast.
- Motley used either tea or coffee for breakfast, depending on his mood.

• William Howitt found great refreshment in both tea and coffee, but he wrote that on his great pedestrian journeys, "Tea would always in a manner almost miraculous banish all my fatigue, and diffuse through my whole frame comfort and exhilaration without any subsequent evil effect. Tea is a wonderful refresher and reviver."

• Justin McCarthy, M. P. the brilliant historian, said that he was a liberal drinker of tea, and that he found it "of immense benefit in keeping off headache, my only malady."

• Harriet Martineau dearly loved her cup of tea.

• Geo. R. Sims says "Tea is my favorite tonic when I am tired or languid."

• An amiable weakness for Afternoon Tea in the course of his daily official duties which was manifested by the late Hon. Wm. L. Strong, the worthy mayor of New York in 1895-1896, furnished the New York newspapers with opportunities for many a good-natured jest and jibe.

• Dr. King Chambers, in a *Manual of Diet in Health and Disease* says of Tea that—"It soothes the nervous system when it is in an uncomfortable state from hunger, fatigue, or mental excitement."

• Florence Nightingale said—"When you see the natural and almost universal craving in English sick for their tea, you cannot but feel that nature knows what she is about. There is nothing yet discovered which is a substitute to the English patient for his or her cup of tea."

• Buckle (the Historian) quotes Dr. Jackson as saying (in 1845) that—"Even for those who have to go through great fatigues, a breakfast of tea and dry bread is more strengthening than one of beefsteak and porter."

• Professor Parkes says—"As an article of diet for soldiers, tea is most useful. The hot infusion, like that of coffee, is potent both against heat and cold; it is useful in great fatigue, especially in hot climates, and also has a great purifying effect upon water. It should form the drink par excellence of the soldiers on service."

• Admiral Inglefield, in 1881, said, that in evidence given before the Artic Committee, of which he was a member, all the witnesses were unanimous in the opinion that spirits taken to keep out cold was a fallacy, and that nothing was more effectual than a good fatty diet, and hot tea or coffee, as a drink. "Seamen who journeyed with me up the shores of Wellington Channel," says the Admiral, "in the artic regions, after one day's experience of rum-drinking, came to the conclusion that Tea, which was the only beverage I used, was much more to be preferred."

• Lord Wolsely, Commander in Chief of the British Army, wrote as follows—"It fell to my lot to lead a brigade through a distant country for more than 600 miles. I fed the men as well as I could, but no one, officer or private, had anything stronger than tea to drink during the expedition. The men had peculiarly hard work to do, and they did it well, and without a murmur. We seem to have left crime and sickness behind us with the "grog," for the conduct of all was most exemplary and no one was ever ill."

• Mr. Winter Blyth, Medical Officer of Health for Marylebone, (London), says in reference to long cycling excursions, and experiments with beer and spirits— "My own experience as to the best drink when on the road is most decidedly in favor of Tea. Tea appears to rouse both the nervous and muscular systems, with, so far as I can discover, no after-depressing effects."

• Edward Payson Weston, the great Pedestrian, finds in Tea and rest the most effective restoratives. He once walked 5000 miles in 100 days, and after each day's work, lectured on "Tea versus Beer."

• C. J. Nichod, late Secretary of the London Athletic Club, writes in his book—*Guide to Athletic Training*, that "Tea is preferable for training purposes, possessing less heating properties and being more digestible than beer or spirits."

Cowper's lines are still classic in their application to English homes and their evening accompaniment, Tea.

"Now stir the fire, and close the shutters fast,
Let fall the curtains, wheel the sofa round,
And while the bubbling and loud-hissing urn
Throws up a steamy column, and the cups
That cheer but not inebriate, wait on each,
So let us welcome peaceful evening in."

QUIZ: THE ABCs OF TEA

Answers to this quiz can be found on page 465.

1. True or False: Orange Pekoe tea is an herbal tea made with orange peel, assam, and bergamot.

2. The following country leads the world in tea consumption:
a. England
b. Ireland
c. China
d. Japan
e. United States

3. Which of the following is not a black tea?
a. Assam
b. Darjeeling
c. Orange Pekoe

d. Ceylon

e. Keemun

4. Which of the following is not a green tea?

a. Sencha

b. Bancha

c. Gunpowder

d. Matcha

e. Chai

5. True or False: All green tea are semi-fermented during manufacture.

6. True or False: Herbal tea comes from the Camellia sinensis plant.

7. Which of the following gentlemen was not associated with the production of the sale of tea?

a. Thomas Garraway

b. Thomas Lipton

c. Thomas Sullivan

d. Dylan Thomas

e. Thomas Twining

8. Tea bricks were used for:

a. Money

b. Food

c. Brewing

d. None of the above

e. All of the above

CHAPTER THREE:

Tea Customs
Around the World

Tea has been an international choice for centuries. From the Far East to the far West, people have been enjoying tea. Customs vary from country to country and we'll take a look of many of those customs, focusing on a few in detail. From an English afternoon cream tea to a Japanese tea ceremony, from the Russian tea houses to the fields of Cameroon, let's take a peak at tea around the world.

> *"Tea to the English is really a picnic indoors."*
> —Alice Walker

TEA PRODUCTION

Tea is produced all over the world. It is produced in Africa, North and South American, Australia, Europe, and Asia...on all the continents but Antarctica! Here are some of the countries currently producing tea:

Argentina	Japan	Rwanda
Australia	Kenya	South Africa
Azores	Madagascar	Sri Lanka
Bangladesh	Malawi	Taiwan
Burundi	Malaysia	Turkey
Cameroon	Mauritius	Uganda
China	Mozambique	United States
Ecuador	Papua	Vietnam
Ethiopia	New	Zaire
India	Guinea	Zimbabwe
Indonesia	Peru	
Iran	Russia	

As tea is consumed on nearly every continent, let's look at some of the customs from each. We'll start with what seems to be an up and coming entry into the tea world: Africa.

Tea in Africa

You might be surprised to discover that tea is a growing industry in African nations.

Tea first appeared in Africa in 1900 when it was brought to the Botanic Gardens at Entebbe in Uganda as an experiment. It proved to be a very successful one. The tea industry became established in Africa with Kenya leading the pack in tea production so far. Many companies have since purchased land for tea plantations in Africa.

African tea-producing countries include:

- Burundi, which produces black tea.
- Kenya, which produces black tea and is the biggest tea producer in Africa at present.

- Madagascar, which produces mostly black tea.
- Malawi, which produces black tea used mostly in blends.
- Mozambique, which produces black tea.
- South Africa, which produces black tea.
- Rwanda, which produces black tea.
- Tanzania, which produces black tea and is another one of the largest tea producers in Africa.
- Uganda, which produces black tea.
- Zaire, which produces black tea.
- Zimbabwe, which produces black tea.

The majority of the tea produced in Africa is exported. In 2006, according to Arun Deshpande, marketing manager of the African agricultural estates company Sasini, total tea production in Africa stood at 682 million pounds, while

local consumption totaled a mere 36.3 million pounds. Despite the statistic, you will find tea is a popular drink all over Africa.

Mint tea is most likely the most popular drink in Morocco, perhaps in all of Northern Africa. If you are offered a glass of mint tea in Northern Africa, it is impolite to turn it down. The more you drink, the better! The making and drinking of mint tea is somewhat ceremonial: Africans take their tea drinking seriously. Try to make a batch for yourself:

6 cups cold, filtered or bottled spring water

8 teaspoons gunpowder green tea

sugar, to taste

1 cup fresh mint leaves

small glasses (not cups) for serving

Bring fresh water to a near boil. Pour a small amount into a teapot to warm and clean the pot. Discard the water. Fill the pot with six cups of water and add the tea in a strainer or infuser. Add the sugar and the fresh mint leaves. Let steep for one to three minutes, but no longer. Discard the tea leaves and prepare to serve the tea for your guests.

To serve the tea in the proper African fashion, pour the tea from shoulder height into a glass. This is done to create a froth on the beverage. Pour the tea back into the pot two to three times in order to stir the tea and mix the sugar thoroughly. This is a ritualistic aspect of the African tea service. Once you have poured the tea back into the pot several times, serve the tea for drinking. It is customary to drink two to three glasses of the hot tea.

In some parts of Africa, dark teas are the beverage of choice. In Egypt, for example, you will find tea everywhere, in coffee shops, on tea stands, and in nearly every home. Tea glasses are small as well, and tea is a daily ritual. However, the tea is cooked on the stove until it is inky black and very strong. Most tea is served with two to three tablespoons of sugar—the sweeter the better. Tea leaves are usually left in the pot, so be careful when you reach the bottom of your glass!

Tea in England

Upon hearing the word tea, many people immediately think of England and afternoon tea. As we have seen, tea has a long-standing tradition in England from the highest drawing rooms to the everyday kitchen tables. Tearooms abound in England, and the afternoon teas at Harrods, the Ritz, Fortnum and Mason's, The Promenade at the Dorchester Hotel and the Conservatory at The Lanesborough are all popular stops for visitors to London. Any of these experiences will be well worth the price, even with a terrible exchange rate!

> *"There are few hours in life more agreeable than the hour dedicated to the ceremony known as afternoon tea."*
>
> —Henry James, The Portrait of a Lady

If you don't have time to pop over the pond for a genuine English cuppa, however, you can re-create the experience at in your own home.

Tea Parties for the Ladies (and Gents)

You will need a few supplies. For a tea selection, choose between any of the following highly recommended teas:

- English Breakfast
- Earl Grey
- Jasmine
- Irish Breakfast

You can also add a selection of herbal teas to complement: chamomile, a fruity tea, or perhaps a mint tea.

Teapots: You can purchase inexpensive, individual teapots online. (For example, see The English Tea Store online at http://www.englishteastore.com/teapots.html for inexpensive—from $3.95 to $60.00—but wonderful colorful teapots at a great value.)

China: Ladies and gentlemen prefer to drink their tea in English china and eat their pastries and finger sandwiches off of china plates. You can start collecting different styles at garage sales, flea markets, through eBay or other online trading companies, and your local antique stores. And don't forget to check out grandma's attic or a great-aunt's china collection. It's always more fun to have a diverse and varied collection of china cups and plates so everyone can compare and contrast their place settings with that of their neighbor's. Trading can get very interesting indeed. You can also get out the polish and prepare the silver tea service if you are lucky enough to have one.

You will also need:

Jugs: For milk and cream.

Sugar cubes: In a china bowl with spoon for serving.

Silverware: Pretty butter knives for spreading jams, creams and other delicious lunch treats are also a wonderful addition, adding color and style; spoons; cake servers for delicious desserts.

Linens: Including a tablecloth, fine linen napkins for each guest.

Napkin rings: For napkins.

Place cards: You can create your own place cards for each guest using cardstock. Simply cut the cardstock into suitably sized place cards. Write each guest's name in calligraphy or with colorful markers on the cardstock and punch a hole through the top of the card. Attach the card with raffia or other decorative string or yarn and wrap around the napkin for a wonderful, homemade place setting.

Flowers and centerpieces: Create centerpieces out of

a teapot and flowers or ivy. Roses are always an appropriate and lovely centerpiece for tea parties. Small posies of pansies are also very nice.

Afternoon English Tea

For a real English tea experience, open with your guests choosing their tea of choice from your menu of available teas, hopefully displayed in a beautiful wooden tea box or wicker basket lined with linens to match your set table.

You can make any or all of the following food choices for your guests:

A variety of finger sandwiches, including but certainly not limited to:

- Egg and cress on rye
- Smoked salmon with capers and cream cheese on pumpernickel
- Any pâté topped with thin slices of cucumber or black olives on wheat bread

- Cucumber sandwiches with cream cheese and mint
- Tuna salad with slice of radish on white bread

Simply remove the crusts of your breads, cut the bread into either two or four even pieces, and make finger sandwiches for all to enjoy. This allows each guest to have a sampling of sandwich treats rather than choosing one full-sized sandwich alone.

Scones: There are many wonderful scone recipes online and in a number of cookbooks. Raisin scones are delicious, as are cranberry scones, plain scones, and buttermilk scones. Be sure to sprinkle a little extra sugar on top!

- Strawberry jam
- Devonshire or Cornish clotted cream (You can order clotted cream online at Britishdelights.com or another online food purveyor of British food goods.)

Follow the sandwiches and scones with a selection of pastries and petit fours. Costco and Sam's Club both sell a delightful selection of petit fours at bargain prices. Other possible dessert treats include lemon bars and shortbread.

If you don't want to serve the whole shebang, you can also do a cream tea. Cream teas are a wonderful treat. Anyone who has visited the Devonshire country-side and had a proper cream tea has tasted a little slice of heaven in England.

Cream Tea

A cream tea cannot be considered a proper cream tea if cream is not served alongside a warm scone straight from the oven. Cream tea means Devonshire clotted cream or Cornish clotted cream. Before milk was pasteurized, milk straight from the cow was left in buckets for hours so that the cream would rise to the surface and could then be skimmed off the top. The cream was then scalded. Scalding was a process whereby the cream was put into large pans and set on top of constantly boiling water. This process would thicken the cream until it developed the consistency of butter. Today clotted cream is made mechanically and the old-fashioned process has been left behind. But it still comes from the West Country of England, where the climate, the soil and the cows come together to form a perfect combination for this amazing treat. For a simple English cream tea, prepare your table and tea as outlined above, but serve:

- Jam
- Butter
- Scones
- Lemon curd
- Clotted cream

An English cream tea is truly a slice of perfection. But you might want to limit your intake to special occasions: It's certainly not a low-calorie treat!

> "Another novelty is the tea party, an extraordinary meal in that, being offered to persons that have already dined well, it supposes neither appetite nor thirst, and has no object but distraction, no basis but delicate enjoyment."
>
> —Jean-Anthelme Brillat-Savarin,
> *The Physiology of Taste*

Tea in Japan

Most Westerners think of tea as a pick-me-up, a morning beverage to be gulped down on the way to work or savored once at your desk or kitchen table. A cup of tea at night is considered a social event or perhaps a way for you to sit back and relax. Most of us drink our tea in a foam to-go cup with a teabag and a little bit of milk and sugar. Or perhaps some honey, squeezed out of a honey-bear with a wedge of lemon thrown in for tartness. However, in Japan, in Buddhist circles, tea is a ritual. Once you experience tea this way, you will never look at your to-go cup in quite the same way. Tea itself is ceremony.

To set the stage for a Japanese Zen tea ceremony, we turn to the words of Okakura Kakuzo and his book, *The Book of Tea: The Schools of Tea*.

Tea is a work of art and needs a master hand to bring out its noblest qualities. We have good and bad tea, as we have good and bad paintings—generally the latter.

There is no single recipe for making the perfect tea, as there are no rules for producing a Titian or a Sesson. Each preparation of the leaves has its individuality, its special affinity with water and heat, its own method of telling a story. The truly beautiful must always be in it. How much do we not suffer through the constant failure of society to recognize this simple and fundamental law of art and life; Lichilai, a Sung poet, has sadly remarked that there were three most deplorable things in the world: the spoiling of fine youths through false education, the degradation of fine art through vulgar admiration, and the utter waste of fine tea through incompetent manipulation.

Like Art, Tea has its periods and its schools. Its evolution may be roughly divided into three main stages: the Boiled Tea, the Whipped Tea, and the Steeped Tea. We moderns belong to the last school. These several methods of appreciating the beverage are indicative of the spirit of the age in which they prevailed. For life is an expression, our unconscious actions the constant betrayal of our innermost thought. Confucius said that "man hideth not." Perhaps we reveal ourselves too

much in small things because we have so little of the
great to conceal. The tiny incidents of daily routine are
as much a commentary of racial ideals as the highest
flight of philosophy or poetry. Even as the difference in
favorite vintage marks the separate idiosyncrasies of
different periods and nationalities of Europe, so the
Tea-ideals characterize the various moods of Oriental
culture. The Cake-tea which was boiled, the
Powdered-tea which was whipped, the Leaf-tea which
was steeped, mark the distinct emotional impulses of
the Tang, the Sung, and the Ming dynasties of China.
If we were inclined to borrow the much-abused terminology of art-classification, we might designate them
respectively, the Classic, the Romantic, and the
Naturalistic schools of Tea.

The tea-plant, a native of southern China, was known
from very early times to Chinese botany and medicine.
It is alluded to in the classics under the various names
of Tou, Tseh, Chung, Kha, and Ming, and was highly

prized for possessing the virtues of relieving fatigue, delighting the soul, strengthening the will, and repairing the eyesight. It was not only administered as an internal dose, but often applied externally in form of paste to alleviate rheumatic pains. The Taoists claimed it as an important ingredient of the elixir of immortality. The Buddhists used it extensively to prevent drowsiness during their long hours of meditation.

By the fourth and fifth centuries, Tea became a favorite beverage among the inhabitants of the Yangtse-Kiang valley. It was about this time that modern ideograph Cha was coined, evidently a corruption of the classic Tou. The poets of the southern dynasties have left some fragments of their fervent adoration of the "froth of the liquid jade." Then emperors used to bestow some rare preparation of the leaves on their high ministers as a reward for eminent services. Yet the method of drinking tea at this stage was primitive in the extreme. The leaves were steamed, crushed in a

mortar, made into a cake, and boiled together with rice,
ginger, salt, orange peel, spices, milk, and sometimes
with onions! The custom obtains at the present day
among the Thibetans and various Mongolian tribes,
who make a curious syrup of these ingredients. The use
of lemon slices by the Russians, who learned to take tea
from the Chinese caravansaries, points to the survival
of the ancient method.

It needed the genius of the Tang dynasty to emanci-
pate Tea from its crude state and lead to its final
idealization. With Luwuh in the middle of the eighth
century we have our first apostle of tea. He was born in
an age when Buddhism, Taoism, and Confucianism
were seeking mutual synthesis. The pantheistic symbolism of the time was urging one to mirror the Universal
in the Particular. Luwuh, a poet, saw in the Tea-service
the same harmony and order which reigned through all
things. In his celebrated work, the "*Chaking*" (The
Holy Scripture of Tea) he formulated the Code of Tea.

He has since been worshipped
as the tutelary god of the
Chinese tea merchants.

The "*Chaking*" consists
of three volumes and ten
chapters. In the first chapter,
Luwuh treats of the nature of
the tea-plant, in the second,
of the implements for gathering the leaves, and in
the third, of the selection of the leaves. According to
him the best quality of the leaves must have "creases
like the leathern boot of Tartar horsemen, curl like the
dewlap of a mighty bullock, unfold like a mist rising
out of a ravine, gleam like a lake touched by a zephyr,
and be wet and soft like fine earth newly swept by
rain."

The fourth chapter is devoted to the enumeration
and description of the twenty-four members of the tea-
equipage, beginning with the tripod brazier and ending

with the bamboo cabinet for containing all these utensils. Here we notice Luwuh's predilection for Taoist
symbolism. Also it is interesting to observe in this connection the influence of tea on Chinese ceramics. The
Celestial porcelain, as is well known, had its origin in
an attempt to reproduce the exquisite shade of jade,
resulting, in the Tang dynasty, in the blue glaze of the
south, and the white glaze of the north. Luwuh considered the blue as the ideal color for the tea-cup, as it
lent additional greenness to the beverage, whereas
the white made it look pinkish and distasteful. It
was because he used cake-tea. Later on, when the tea
masters of Sung took to the powdered tea, they preferred heavy bowls of blue-black and dark brown. The
Mings, with their steeped tea, rejoiced in light ware of
white porcelain.

  In the fifth chapter, Luwuh describes the method of
making tea. He eliminates all ingredients except salt.
He dwells also on the much-discussed question of the

choice of water and the degree of boiling it. According to him, the mountain spring is the best, the river water and the spring water come next in the order of excellence. There are three stages of boiling: the first boil is when the little bubbles like the eye of fishes swim on the surface; the second boil is when the bubbles are like crystal beads rolling in a fountain; the third boil is when the billows surge wildly in the kettle. The Cake-tea is roasted before the fire until it becomes soft like a baby's arm and is shredded into powder between pieces of fine paper. Salt is put in the first boil, then tea in the second boil.

At the third boil, a dipperful of cold water is poured into the kettle to settle the tea and revive the "youth of the water." Then the beverage was poured into cups and drunk. O nectar! The filmy leaflet hung like scaly clouds in a serene sky or floated like water lilies on emerald streams. It was of such a beverage that Lotung, a Tang poet, wrote: "The first cup moistens my lips and throat, the second cup breaks my loneliness, the third cup searches my barren entrails but to find therein some five thousand volumes of odd ideographs. The fourth cup raises a slight perspiration—all the wrong of life passes away through my pores. At the fifth cup I am purified; the sixth cup calls me to the realms of the immortals. The seventh cup—ah, but I could take no more! I only feel the breath of cool wind that rises in my sleeves. Where is Horaisan? Let me ride on this sweet breeze and waft away thither."

The remaining chapters of the "Chaking" treat of the vulgarity of the ordinary methods of tea-drinking, a historical summary of illustrious tea-drinkers, the famous tea plantations of China, the possible variations of the tea-service and illustrations of the tea-utensils.

The last is unfortunately lost.

The appearance of the "Chaking" must have created a considerable sensation at

the time. Luwuh was befriended by the Emperor
Taisung (763-779), and his fame attracted many follow-
ers. Some exquisites were said to have been able to
detect the tea made by Luwuh from that of his disciples. One mandarin has his name immortalized by his
failure to appreciate the tea of this great master.

In the Sung dynasty, the whipped tea came into fashion and created the second school of Tea. The leaves
were ground to fine powder in a small stone mill, and
the preparation was whipped in hot water by a delicate
whisk made of split bamboo. The new process led to
some change in the tea-equipage of Luwuh, as well as
in the choice of leaves. Salt was discarded forever. The
enthusiasm of the Sung people for tea knew no
bounds. Epicures vied with each other in discovering
new varieties, and regular tournaments were held to
decide their superiority. The Emperor Kiasung (1101-
1124), who was too great an artist to be a well-behaved
monarch, lavished his treasures on the attainment of

rare species. He himself wrote a dissertation on the twenty kinds of tea, among which he prizes the "white tea" as of the rarest and finest quality.

The tea-ideal of the Sungs differed from the Tangs even as their notion of life differed. They sought to actualize what their predecessors tried to symbolize. To the Neo-Confucian mind the cosmic law was not reflected in the phenomenal world, but the phenomenal world was the cosmic law itself. Aeons were but moments—Nirvana always within grasp. The Taoist conception that immortality lay in the eternal change permeated all their modes of thought. It was the process, not the deed, which was interesting. It was the completing, not the completion, which was really vital. Man came thus at once face to face with nature. A new meaning grew into the art of life. The tea began to be not a poetical pastime, but one of the methods of self-realization. Wangyucheng eulogized tea as "flooding his soul like a direct appeal, that its delicate bitterness

reminded him of the aftertaste of a good counsel."
Sotumpa wrote of the strength of the immaculate purity
in tea which defied corruption as a truly virtuous man.
Among the Buddhists, the southern Zen sect, which
incorporated so much of Taoist doctrines, formulated
an elaborate ritual of tea. The monks gathered before
the image of Bodhi Dharma and drank tea out of a single bowl with the profound formality of a holy sacra-
ment. It was this Zen ritual which finally developed
into the Tea-ceremony of Japan in the fifteenth century.

Unfortunately the sudden outburst of the Mongol
tribes in the thirteenth century which resulted in the
devastation and conquest of China under the barbaric
rule of the Yuen Emperors destroyed all the fruits of
Sung culture. The native dynasty of the Mings which
attempted re-nationalization in the middle of the fifteenth century was harassed by internal troubles, and
China again fell under the alien rule of the Manchus in
the seventeenth century. Manners and customs changed

to leave no vestige of the former times. The powdered tea is entirely forgotten. We find a Ming commentator at loss to recall the shape of the tea whisk mentioned in one of the Sung classics. Tea is now taken by steeping the leaves in hot water in a bowl or cup. The reason why the Western world is innocent of the older method of drinking tea is explained by the fact that Europe knew it only at the close of the Ming dynasty.

To the latter-day Chinese, tea is a delicious beverage, but not an ideal. The long woes of his country have robbed him of the zest for the meaning of life. He has become modern, that is to say, old and disenchanted. He has lost that sublime faith in illusions which constitutes the eternal youth and vigor of the poets and ancients. He is an eclectic and politely accepts the traditions of the universe.

He toys with Nature, but does not condescend to conquer or worship her. His Leaf-tea is often wonderful with its flower-like aroma, but the romance of the Tang and Sung ceremonials are not to be found in his cup.

Japan, which followed closely on the footsteps of Chinese civilization, has known the tea in all its three stages. As early as the year 729 we read of the Emperor Shomu giving tea to one hundred monks at his palace in Nara. The leaves were probably imported by our ambassadors to the Tang Court and prepared in the way then in fashion. In 801, the monk Saicho brought back some seeds and planted them in Yeisan. Many tea-gardens are heard of in succeeding centuries, as well as the delight of the aristocracy and priesthood in the beverage. The Sung tea reached us in 1191 with the return of Yeisai-zenji, who went there to study the southern Zen school. The new seeds which he carried home were successfully planted in three places, one of which, the Uji district near Kioto, bears still the name of producing the best tea in the world. The southern Zen spread with marvelous rapidity, and with it the tea-ritual and the tea-ideal of the Sung. By the fifteenth

century, under the patronage of the Shogun, Ashikaga-
Voshinasa, the tea ceremony is fully constituted and
made into an independent and secular performance.

Since then, Teaism has been fully established in
Japan. The use of the steeped tea of later China is comparatively recent among us, being only known since the
middle of the seventeenth century. It has replaced the
powdered tea in ordinary consumption, though the
latter still continues to hold its place as the tea of teas.

It is in the Japanese tea ceremony that we see the cul-
mination of tea-ideals. Our successful resistance of the
Mongol invasion in 1281 had enabled us to carry on the
Sung movement so disastrously cut off in China itself
through the nomadic inroad. Tea with us became more
than an idealization of the form of drinking; it is a religion of the art of life. The beverage grew to be an
excuse for the worship of purity and refinement, a
sacred function at which the host and guest joined to
produce for that occasion the utmost beatitude of the

mundane. The tea-room was an oasis in the dreary waste of existence where weary travelers could meet to drink from the common spring of art-appreciation. The ceremony was an improvised drama whose plot was woven about the tea, the flowers, and the paintings. Not a color to disturb the tone of the room, not a sound to mar the rhythm of things, not a gesture to obtrude on the harmony, not a word to break the unity of the surroundings, all movements to be performed simply and naturally—such were the aims of the tea-ceremony. And strangely enough it was often successful.

In Japan, the tea ceremony is known as *Chanoyu*, which translates to "hot water for tea." *Chanoyu* is a single ceremony, while *cha-ji* or *chakai* (translated as "tea meeting") indicates a full tea ceremony with a light meal involved. *Chanoyu* is based on the principles of respect, harmony, purity, and tranquility. The tea ceremony is traditionally performed in a tearoom. To see a traditional Japanese tearoom, you can visit the webpage

of Washington and Lee University's new Japanese
Tearoom. This amazing re-creation was built in the
Watson Pavilion on their campus, where it provides
the environment for the study of Chadÿ, the Way of
Tea. It also provides the community in Lexington,
Virginia with a center for "cultural activity relating to
the arts of Japan."

Everyone in the tearoom is of equal status, and
great respect is paid to each individual. There is nothing
in the tearoom that isn't a vital part of the ceremony,
and careful, respectful attention is paid to every detail.
Everything in the tearoom must contribute to the
enjoyable experience of each participant. From
Japanese tea flowers to the tatami mats on the floor,
from the scrolls on the walls to the tea bowls themselves, every detail is carefully attended to.

The procedures for the tea ceremony are to be precisely maintained. Each moment if is of equal importance and the steps of the ceremony are to be followed

in exactly the right order. Each moment is to be savored and executed meditatively, as the ceremony flows like water. The Way of Tea is the way of life itself. The steps of the tea ceremony are as follows.

Guests are greeted and taken into the tearoom. Often they are first taken through a garden in order to take a moment before entering the ceremonial room itself and leave the outside world behind.

Each participant must take a seat, and a light snack is served. A kettle is set on the brazier to boil the water. The equipment for the tea ceremony is then brought over so that it can begin. The first item the host brings over is the tea bowl containing a napkin, a whisk, a tea scoop and a tea caddy. He then brings over a bowl for the waste water. This bowl will hold a lid rest and a water ladle.

The lid rest will be situated near the brazier and kettle with the water ladle resting on the top of it. The host begins.

The napkin is used to wipe the tea scoop and the tea caddy. The cleaning of the scoop and caddy lets the guests know the great care the host takes with his service, and how important are the qualities of purity, cleanliness and respect. Remember, the tea ceremony is a meditation itself so every action is taken with intense concentration as the host moves into the Way of Tea. Each piece of equipment used in the ritual is cleaned precisely in the presence of the guests. The utensils are then placed in the exact order they are to be used. Now the tea can be made.

Chanoyu is made up of four principles: *wa*—harmony, *kei*— respect, *sei*—purity, and *jaku*—tranquility.

The tea used in the tea ceremony is usually matcha, a green tea, and must be whipped. The host picks up the tea caddy in his left hand and the scoop in his right, and scoops tea into the tea bowl from the tea caddy. Water is added to make a paste, until the correct consistency is achieved. The tea is whisked and ritually turned in a precise manner. Then it is passed to the first guest, who bows, picks up the bowl and gestures respectfully to the next guest to indicate he is going to drink. He bows again at the host and then drinks from the bowl. He drinks from the side of the bowl, takes a few sips, ritually wipes the bowl with his napkin and passes the bowl to the next guest. And so the ceremony goes.

The process is repeated for all the guests. When the last guest has had tea, the host ritually cleans the tea bowl. The Way of Tea is just one "way" in Japan. Other traditions that have been made into art forms include the Way of Flowers, the Way of Incense, the Way of Calligraphy, the Way of Poetry (haiku), the Way of the Samurai.

To further understand the Way of Tea, we can turn to Okakura Kakuzo's chapter in *The Book of Tea* on the Way of Flowers:

In the trembling grey of a spring dawn, when the birds were whispering in mysterious cadence among the trees, have you not felt that they were talking to their mates about the flowers? Surely with mankind the appreciation of flowers must have been coeval with the poetry of love. Where better than in a flower, sweet in its unconsciousness, fragrant because of its silence, can we image the unfolding of a virgin soul? The primeval man in offering the first garland to his maiden thereby transcended the brute. He became human in thus rising above the crude necessities of nature. He entered the realm of art when he perceived the subtle use of the useless.

In joy or sadness, flowers are our constant friends. We eat, drink, sing, dance, and flirt with them. We wed and christen with flowers. We dare not die without them. We have worshipped with the lily, we have meditated with the lotus, we have charged in battle array with the rose and the chrysanthemum. We have even attempted to speak in the language of flowers. How could we live without them? It frightens one to conceive of a world bereft of their presence. What solace do they not bring to the bedside of the sick, what a light of bliss to the darkness of weary spirits? Their serene tenderness restores to us our waning confidence in the universe even as the intent gaze of a beautiful child recalls our lost hopes. When we are laid low in the dust it is they who linger in sorrow over our graves.

Sad as it is, we cannot conceal the fact that in spite of our companionship with flowers we have not risen very far above the brute. Scratch the sheepskin and the wolf within us will soon show his teeth. It has been said that a man at ten is an animal, at twenty a lunatic, at thirty a failure, at forty a fraud, and at fifty a criminal. Perhaps he becomes a criminal because he has never ceased to be an animal. Nothing is real to us but hunger, nothing sacred except our own desires. Shrine after shrine has crumbled before our eyes; but one altar is forever preserved, that whereon we burn incense to the supreme idol—ourselves. Our god is great, and money is his Prophet! We devastate nature in

order to make sacrifice to him. We boast that we have con-
quered Matter and forget that it is Matter that has enslaved
us. What atrocities do we not perpetrate in the name of
culture and refinement!

Tell me, gentle flowers, teardrops of the stars, standing in
the garden, nodding your heads to the bees as they sing of
the dews and the sunbeams, are you aware of the fearful
doom that awaits you? Dream on, sway and frolic while you
may in the gentle breezes of summer. To-morrow a ruthless
hand will close around your throats. You will be wrenched,
torn asunder limb by limb, and borne away from your quiet
homes. The wretch, she may be passing fair. She may say
how lovely you are while her fingers are still moist with
your blood. Tell me, will this be kindness? It may be your
fate to be imprisoned in the hair of one whom you know to
be heartless or to be thrust into the buttonhole of one who
would not dare to look you in the face were you a man. It
may even be your lot to be confined in some narrow vessel
with only stagnant water to quench the maddening thirst

that warns of ebbing life.

Flowers, if you were in the land of the Mikado, you might some time meet a dread personage armed with scissors and a tiny saw. He would call himself a Master of Flowers. He would claim the rights of a doctor and you would instinctively hate him, for you know a doctor always seeks to prolong the troubles of his victims. He would cut, bend, and twist you into those impossible positions which he thinks it proper that you should assume. He would contort your muscles and dislocate your bones like any osteopath. He would burn you with red-hot coals to stop your bleeding, and thrust wires into you to assist your circulation. He would diet you with salt, vinegar, alum, and sometimes, vitriol. Boiling water would be poured on your feet when you seemed ready to faint.

It would be his boast that he could keep life within you for two or more weeks longer than would have been possible without his treatment. Would you not have preferred to have been killed at once when you were first captured? What were the crimes you must have committed during your past incarnation to warrant such punishment in this?

The wanton waste of flowers among Western communities is even more appalling than the way they are treated by Eastern Flower Masters. The number of flowers cut daily to adorn the ballrooms and banquet-tables of Europe and America, to be thrown away on the morrow, must be something enormous; if strung together they might garland a continent. Beside this utter carelessness of life, the guilt of the Flower-Master becomes insignificant. He, at least, respects the economy of nature, selects his victims with careful foresight, and after death does honor to their remains. In the West the display of flowers seems to be a part of the pageantry of wealth—the fancy of a moment. Whither do they all go, these flowers, when the revelry is over? Nothing is more pitiful than to see a faded flower remorselessly flung upon a dung heap.

Why were the flowers born so beautiful and yet so hapless? Insects can sting, and even the meekest of beasts will fight when brought to bay. The birds whose plumage is sought to deck some bonnet can fly from its pursuer, the furred animal whose coat you covet for your own may hide at your approach. Alas! The only flower known to have wings is the butterfly; all others stand helpless before the destroyer. If they shriek in their death agony their cry never reaches our hardened ears. We are ever brutal to those who love and serve us in silence, but the time may come when, for our cruelty, we shall be deserted by these best friends of ours. Have you not noticed that the wild flowers are becoming scarcer every year? It may be that their wise men have told them to depart till man become more human. Perhaps they have migrated to heaven.

Much may be said in favor of him who cultivates plants. The man of the pot is far more humane than he of the scissors. We watch with delight his concern about water and sunshine, his feuds with parasites, his horror of frosts, his anxiety when the buds come slowly, his rapture when the leaves attain their luster. In the East the art of floriculture is a very ancient one, and the loves of a poet and his favorite plant have often been recorded in story and song. With the development of ceramics during the Tang and Sung dynasties we hear of wonderful receptacles made to hold plants, not pots, but jeweled palaces. A special attendant was detailed to wait upon each flower and to wash its leaves with soft brushes made of rabbit hair. It has been written ("Pingtse," by Yuenchunlang) that the peony should be bathed by a handsome maiden in full costume, that a winter-plum should be watered by a pale, slender monk. In Japan, one of the most popular of the No-dances, the Hachinoki, composed during the Ashikaga period, is based upon the story of an impoverished knight, who, on a freezing night, in lack of fuel for a fire, cuts his cherished plants in order to entertain a wandering friar. The friar is in reality no other than Hojo-Tokiyori, the Haroun-Al-Raschid of our tales, and the sacrifice is not without its reward. This opera never fails to draw tears from a Tokyo audience, even today.

Great precautions were taken for the preservation of

delicate blossoms. Emperor Huensung, of the Tang Dynasty, hung tiny golden bells on the branches in his garden to keep off the birds. It was he who went off in the springtime with his court musicians to gladden the flowers with soft music. A quaint tablet, which tradition ascribes to Yoshitsune, the hero of our Arthurian legends, is still extant in one of the Japanese monasteries (Sumadera, near Kobe). It is a notice put up for the protection of a certain wonderful plum-tree, and appeals to us with the grim humor of a warlike age. After referring to the beauty of the blossoms, the inscription says: "Whoever cuts a single branch of this tree shall forfeit a finger therefore." Would that such laws could be enforced nowadays against those who wantonly destroy flowers and mutilate objects of art!

Yet even in the case of pot flowers we are inclined to sus-pect the selfishness of man. Why take the plants from their homes and ask them to bloom mid strange surroundings? Is it not like asking the birds to sing and mate cooped up in cages? Who knows but that the orchids feel stifled by the artificial heat in your conservatories and hopelessly long for a glimpse of their own Southern skies?

The ideal lover of flowers is he who visits them in their native haunts, like Taoyuenming (all celebrated Chinese poets and philosophers), who sat before a broken bamboo fence in converse with the wild chrysanthemum, or Linwosing, losing himself amid mysterious fragrance as he wandered in the twilight among the plum-blossoms of the Western Lake. 'Tis said that Chowmushih slept in a boat so that his dreams might mingle with those of the lotus. It was the same spirit which moved the Empress Komio, one of our most renowned Nara sovereigns, as she sang: "If I pluck thee, my hand will defile thee, O flower! Standing in the meadows as thou art, I offer thee to the Buddhas of the past, of the present, of the future."

However, let us not be too sentimental. Let us be less luxurious but more magnificent. Said Laotse: "Heaven and earth are pitiless." Said Kobodaishi: "Flow, flow, flow, flow, the current of life is ever onward. Die, die, die, die, death comes to all." Destruction faces us wherever we turn. Destruction below and above, destruction behind and before. Change is the only Eternal—why not as welcome Death as Life? They are but counterparts one of the other— The Night and Day of Brahma. Through the disintegration of the old, re-creation becomes possible. We have worshipped Death, the relentless goddess of mercy, under many different names. It was the shadow of the All-devouring that the Gheburs greeted in the fire. It is the icy purism of the sword-soul before which Shinto-Japan prostrates herself even to-day. The mystic fire consumes our weakness, the sacred sword cleaves the bondage of desire. From our ashes springs the phoenix of celestial hope, out of the freedom comes a higher realization of manhood.

Why not destroy flowers if thereby we can evolve new forms ennobling the world idea? We only ask them to join in our sacrifice to the beautiful. We shall atone for the deed by consecrating ourselves to Purity and Simplicity. Thus reasoned the teamasters when they established the Cult of Flowers.

Anyone acquainted with the ways of our tea- and flower-masters must have noticed the religious veneration with which they regard flowers. They do not cull at random, but carefully select each branch or spray with an eye to the artistic composition they have in mind. They would be ashamed should they chance to cut more than were absolutely necessary. It may be remarked in this connection that they always associate the leaves, if there be any, with the flower, for the object is to present the whole beauty of plant life. In this respect, as in many others, their method differs from that pursued in Western countries. Here we are apt to see only the flower stems, heads as it were, without body, stuck promiscuously into a vase.

When a tea-master has arranged a flower to his satisfaction he will place it on the tokonoma, the place of honor in a Japanese room. Nothing else will be placed near it which might interfere with its effect, not even a painting, unless there be some special aesthetic reason for the combination.

It rests there like an enthroned prince, and the guests or disciples on entering the room will salute it with a profound bow before making their addresses to the host. Drawings from masterpieces are made and published for the edification of amateurs. The amount of literature on the subject is quite voluminous. When the flower fades, the master tenderly consigns it to the river or carefully buries it in the ground. Monuments are sometimes erected to their memory.

The birth of the Art of Flower Arrangement seems to be simultaneous with that of Teaism in the fifteenth century. Our legends ascribe the first flower arrangement to those early Buddhist saints who gathered the flowers strewn by the storm and, in their infinite solicitude for all living things, placed them in vessels of water. It is said that Soami, the great painter and connoisseur of the court of Ashikaga-Yoshimasa, was one of the earliest adepts at it. Juko, the tea-master, was one of his pupils, as was also Senno, the founder of the house of Ikenobo, a family as illustrious in the annals of flowers as was that of the Kanos in painting.

With the perfecting of the tea-ritual under Rikiu, in the latter part of the sixteenth century, flower arrangement also attains its full growth. Rikiu and his successors, the celebrated Oda- wuraka, Furuka-Oribe, Koyetsu, Kobori-Enshiu, Katagiri- Sekishiu, vied with each other in forming new combinations. We must remember, however, that the flower-worship of the tea-masters formed only a part of their aesthetic ritual, and was not a distinct religion by itself. A flower arrangement, like the other works of art in the tea-room, was subordinated to the total scheme of decoration. Thus Sekishiu ordained that white plum blossoms should not be made use of when snow lay in the garden. "Noisy" flowers were relentlessly banished from the tea-room. A flower arrangement by a tea-master loses its significance if removed from the place for which it was originally intended, for its lines and proportions have been specially worked out with a view to its surroundings.

The adoration of the flower for its own sake begins with the rise of "Flower-Masters," toward the middle of the

*seventeenth century. It now becomes independent of the
tea-room and knows no law save that the vase imposes on
it. New conceptions and methods of execution now become
possible, and many were the principles and schools resulting
therefrom. A writer in the middle of the last century said he
could count over one hundred different schools of flower
arrangement. Broadly speaking, these divide themselves into
two main branches, the Formalistic and the Naturalesque.
The Formalistic schools, led by the Ikenobos, aimed at a
classic idealism corresponding to that of the Kano-academi-
cians. We possess records of arrangements by the early
masters of the school which almost reproduce the flower
paintings of Sansetsu and Tsunenobu. The Naturalesque
school, on the other hand, accepted nature as its model, only
imposing such modifications of form as conduced to the
expression of artistic unity. Thus we recognise in its works
the same impulses which formed the Ukiyoe and Shijo
schools of painting.*

It would be interesting, had we time, to enter more fully

than it is now possible into the laws of composition and detail formulated by the various flower-masters of this period, showing, as they would, the fundamental theories which governed Tokugawa decoration. We find them referring to the Leading Principle (Heaven), the Subordinate Principle (Earth), the Reconciling Principle (Man), and any flower arrangement which did not embody these principles was considered barren and dead. They also dwelt much on the importance of treating a flower in its three different aspects, the Formal, the Semi-Formal, and the Informal. The first might be said to represent flowers in the stately costume of the ballroom, the second in the easy elegance of afternoon dress, the third in the charming deshabille of the boudoir.

Our personal sympathies are with the flower-arrangements of the tea-master rather than with those of the flower-master. The former is art in its proper setting and appeals to us on account of its true intimacy with life. We should like to call this school the Natural in contradistinction to the Naturalesque and Formalistic schools. The tea-master deems his duty ended with the selection of the flowers, and leaves them to tell their own story. Entering a tea-room in late winter, you may see a slender spray of wild cherries in combination with a budding camellia; it is an echo of departing winter coupled with the prophecy of spring. Again, if you go into a noon-tea on some irritatingly hot summer day, you may discover in the darkened coolness of the tokonoma a single lily in a hanging vase; dripping with dew, it seems to smile at the foolishness of life.

A solo of flowers is interesting, but in a concerto with painting and sculpture the combination becomes entrancing. Sekishiu once placed some water-plants in a flat receptacle to suggest the vegetation of lakes and marshes, and on the wall above he hung a painting by Soami of wild ducks flying in the air. Shoha, another tea-master, combined a poem on the Beauty of Solitude by the Sea with a bronze incense burner in the form of a fisherman's hut and some wild flowers of the beach. One of the guests has recorded that he felt in the whole composition the breath of waning autumn.

Flower stories are endless. We shall recount but one more. In the sixteenth century the morning-glory was as yet a rare plant with us. Rikiu had an entire garden planted with it, which he cultivated with assiduous care. The fame of his convolvuli reached the ear of the Taiko, and he expressed a desire to see them, in consequence of which Rikiu invited him to a morning tea at his house. On the appointed day Taiko walked through the garden, but nowhere could he see any vestige of the convulvus.

The ground had been leveled and strewn with fine pebbles and sand.

With sullen anger the despot entered the tea-room, but a sight waited him there which completely restored his humour. On the tokonoma, in a rare bronze of Sung work-manship, lay a single morning-glory—the queen of the whole garden!

In such instances we see the full significance of the Flower Sacrifice. Perhaps the flowers appreciate the full significance of it. They are not cowards, like men. Some flowers glory in death—certainly the Japanese cherry blossoms do, as they freely surrender themselves to the winds. Anyone who has stood before the fragrant avalanche at Yoshino or Arashiyama must have realized this. For a moment they hover like bejewelled clouds and dance above the crystal streams; then, as they sail away on the laughing waters, they seem to say: "Farewell, O Spring! We are on to eternity."

> *"Find yourself a cup of tea; the teapot is behind you. Now tell me about hundreds of things."*
>
> —Saki

Tea in Russia

Would you find it hard to believe that tea ranks with vodka as the most popular beverages in Russia? Tea is associated in Russia with social gathering, with warmth and comfort, good conversation and friends. Russians are passionate people and, yes, they are as passionate about their tea as they are about their vodka. Russians like both green tea and black tea, though the preferred way of drinking black tea is without milk, and in glasses, which are usually quite ornate, with metal handles. The tea can be sweetened with sugar, honey, or even jam. Sometimes the sweetener is put in the mouth before drinking the tea; sometimes the sweetener is added directly to the tea. Russians love their tea: it wards off the cold winter temperatures and brings friends together.

> *"Love and scandal are the best sweeteners of tea."*
> —Henry Fielding, *"Love in Several Masques"*

The history of how tea came to Russia is somewhat murky. There are a few different theories to choose from. One legend tells us that two Cossacks brought news of tea to Russia after a trip to China in the mid-sixteenth century. Or perhaps tea was a seventeenth century addition to Russian culture when a gift was bestowed upon the court of Czar Alexis. But then, it might have been a diplomatic gift from Altyun-Khan, ruler of Mongolia to Russian Tsar Michael Fedorovich in 1638. Whatever the story, it does appear that Russia first started drinking tea in the seventeenth century.

One popular tea that people drink all over the world is Russian Caravan Tea, a strong and smoky black tea. This tea is named after the Russian Tea Caravans of the seventeenth century that delivered tea from China to Russia. Caravans made the round trip journey to eastern China and back over a period of sixteen months, arriving in the Russian capital with chests of tea. It was one of the most difficult routes travelers of the world have ever known: 11,000 miles across rough terrain, with horses and camels laden with tea. The overland trade caravans made the trip for hundreds of years, only ceasing when the TransSiberian Railroad was completed in 1900.

Russia's contribution to the world of tea is the samovar, which came into fashion in the mid eighteenth century. The samovar is a metal container used to boil water, traditionally for tea. They are conventionally heated with fire over charcoal or another heating agent, and they have a pipe that runs up the middle through which fuel usually runs in order to keep the water in the surrounding urn very hot. There is an attachment at the top for placing a teapot filled with tea. Russians like their tea extremely strong, so there is a tap on the side of the samovar from which the hot water can be drawn. It is then added to the tea in the teapot to dilute the tea. This tea concentrate is called zavarka. The samovar can be left on for hours, providing continual tea availability. Russian tea is all about the zavarka. The right concentrate must be made in order for the tea to be maximally enjoyed. Today, one can purchase electric samovars. Old-fashioned samovars can still be found in some Russian households around the globe but such samovars are becoming a thing of the past.

> *"Ecstasy is a glass full of tea and a piece of sugar in the mouth."*
>
> —Aleksandr Pushkin

Tea in China

In China, tea is a daily habit. Although the Chinese produce an enormous quantity of black tea, green tea seems to be the drink of choice by most. The Chinese consider five categories of tea:

- Black tea
- Green tea
- Oolong tea (or Wulong tea)
- Scented tea
- Compressed tea

Scented teas are scented with flowers such as jasmine and magnolia, while compressed teas are black teas shaped into bricks.

Tea is an integral part of life in China and many people drink tea all day long. As in Japan, there is a traditional Chinese tea ceremony. Though it is slightly less formal than the Japanese ritual, it too is a meditative practice. Special teapots are used for the tea ritual: these teapots are known as Yixing stoneware pots and can be traced back to the 1500s. The pots are made from unglazed clay, which can take on a glazed look over the years as the oils from the tea leach into the pot itself. Yixing teapots are popular with collectors of teapots.

When using a Yixing teapot, one should only use one kind of tea per pot. The clay of the pots tends to pick up the oils and flavors of the tea and mixing teas will interfere with the enjoyment of your tea.

In recent years, Starbucks has made a move to introduce their coffees into China. Though China is the birthplace of brewed tea and the Chinese have been drinking tea daily for centuries, the coffee market is beginning to take hold. It will be interesting to see what happens to tea as the global marketplace grows!

Tea in Australia

Australia invented some tea rituals all their own. According to the website for Upton Tea, Australian sheep farmers boiled water for tea in a pot they call a billy can. They'd throw in some tea leaves and let the tea simmer while they had their lunch. They would then put in a generous helping of sugar to sweeten the strong brew. The farmer would then drink his fill, but leave some water in the billycan to further steep as he finished a day's work. When he arrived home that night, he had a powerfully steeped brew that had been working for him all day long.

According to the Australian Food and Grocery Council:

- Australians recommend each person drink five cups of tea each day for optimum antioxidant levels.
- In Australia, 83 percent of households use teabags.

- On average, 600 teabags are used per household each year.
- 22 million cups of tea are consumed every in Australia, 80 percent of which are brewed from teabags.
- 68 percent of Australians have their tea with milk, but only 38 percent prefer sugar in their tea.
- Tea accounts for 18 percent of all beverages consumed in Australia.

Tea in North and South America

Tea is making another appearance in the United States after a long and quiet period. Specialty tea businesses are springing up, trying to capture the interests of an established market as well as spur an interest in those who haven't yet found the joy of tea.

In Charleston, South Carolina, The Charleston Tea Plantation (America's only producer of black tea) is growing tea for profit. Apparently, the tea plant,

Camellia sinensis is a distant cousin of the giant magnolia trees that grow along the Southeast Coastal Plains,
making South Carolina a good place to grow tea.

According to the Bigelow tea website: "The
Charleston Tea Plantation continues to be open to the
public. We have recently passed our first anniversary
since our Grand Reopening on May 10, 2007.
Charleston Tea Plantation has become a 'must see' for
all those who are visiting the greater Charleston
area....Over the past year we have welcomed tens of
thousands of visitors who have come to see the unique
splendor of the farm including the breathtaking views
in all directions."

It certainly sounds like a fun place to visit. The only
other tea plantations to date in the United States can be
found in Hawaii, where a small number of farmers are
bringing tea production back. Tea production is gaining
great strength in Hawaii and it's hoped the tea can make
up for the recent years' decline in the sugar crops.

In South America, you can find tea plantations in Argentina, Ecuador, Brazil and Peru. All produce black teas, primarily for export. English influence in the nineteenth century has left the custom of lonche in Peru. Lonche is essentially afternoon tea, and friends and family gather to eat together and share tea. And far, far to the south, in Patagonia, you can find Welsh tea customs followed in the small town of Gaiman, which was settled by the Welsh at the end of the nineteenth century. The town's traditional Welsh tea is accompanied by pastry, cakes and treats.

From the tip of South America to the far north in Russia, tea has found its way into the hearts and homes, into the nooks and crannies of our world.

QUIZ: TEA CUSTOMS AROUND THE WORLD

Answers to this quiz can be found on page 469.

1. True or false: Tea is produced on every continent in the world.

2. True or false: African mint tea is always served cold.

3. The following is not customarily served at an English cream tea:
a. Strawberry jam
b. Scones
c. Milk and sugar
d. Butter
e. Whipped cream

4. Clotted cream is made:
a. In the West Country of England.

b. All over the world.

a. In Australian sheep-herding country.

a. In factories in New York City.

5. Which of the following statement is true of the Japanese tea ceremony?

a. It is a meditation.

b. There are precise rules and procedures to follow

c. The ceremony takes place outside in a tea garden

d. a and b

e. a and c

6. True or false: There is essentially no difference between the Japanese and Chinese tea ceremonies.

7. True or false. The United States is one of the top producers of tea.

8. True or false: Australians prefer loose leaf tea to teabags.

Chapter Four:

The Health Benefits of Tea

It might be a tasty drink, a pick-me-up, and a relaxing break in the day, but is tea actually good for you? From its first appearance as a brewed beverage, tea has been associated with good health. Today, research confirms what tea drinkers have instinctively known for years: Tea is has the potential to be very good for you. Green tea, especially, seems to have wonderful health benefits. Tea is rich in polyphenols, tannin, and flavanoids (see below), fluoride, and vitamins C, K, and B. As few as four cups of tea a day may have a positive impact on your health. Herbal teas are also consumed for their positive impact on health. Just the process of sitting quietly with a warm cup of tea is good for you: It can act as an instant stress reliever! However, lest you start ingesting mega doses of tea on a daily basis, it should be stressed that while research is certainly appears to support the long-held beliefs that tea is a wonder-drink, there is still a tremendous amount of research to be done. So please, drink up!

But be aware that tea will not solve all your health problems and certainly does not take the place of a qualified personal physician.

> *"Tea is drunk to forget the din of the world."*
>   —T'ien Yiheng

Remember Garraway's tea circular from chapter one? Garraway claimed:

The drink is declared to be most wholesome, preserving in perfect health until extreme old age. The particular virtues are these; It maketh the body active and lusty. It helpeth the headache, giddiness and heaviness thereof It removeth the obstructions of the spleen. It is very good against the stone and gravel, cleaning the kidneys and ureters, being drank with virgin's honey, instead of sugar. It taketh away the difficulty of breathing, opening obstructions. It is good against tipitude, distillations, and cleareth the sight. It removeth lassitude, and cleanseth and purifieth acrid humors, and a hot liver. It is good against crudities, strengthening the weakness of the ventricle, or stomach, causing good appetite and digestion, and particularly for men of corpulent body, and such as are great eaters of flesh. It vanquisheth heavy dreams, easeth the frame, and strengtheneth the memory. It overcometh superfluous sleep, and prevents sleepiness in general; a draught of the infusion being taken, so that without trouble, whole nights may be spent in study, without hurt to the body, in that it moderately healeth and bindeth the mouth of the stomach. It prevents and cures agues, surfets, and fevers, by infusing a fit quantity of the leaf, thereby provoking a most gentle vomit and breathing of the pores, and hath been given with wonderful success.

Those are some very strong claims. Let's take a look at what scientists, doctors and naturopaths are saying more than 300 years later!

Green, Black or Oolong?

Tea has been in the news quite a lot recently as medical researchers talk about the benefits of antioxidants. Whether you have a cup of black, green or oolong tea, you will be ingesting polyphenols, which give tea its antioxidant properties. So what are polyphenols and antioxidants?

Polyphenols are antioxidant phytochemicals, which basically means they are chemicals found in plants. An antioxidant is a substance (such as vitamin C) that inhibits oxidation—they are molecules that slow or stop other molecules from oxidizing. So what's wrong with oxygen, you might ask? After all, we need oxygen to live! Well, there are two faces to oxygen: one is good, the other can be harmful. We obviously need to breathe oxygen in order to life: This is good. However, when oxidation occurs in molecules, it can produce free radicals—which might sound like freedom fighters from the sixties, but which are actually catalysts for reactions that can cause damage on the cellular level. In other words, this aspect of oxygen is a problem because it can combine with anything in the body, oxidize it, and promote damage to cell membranes, DNA, and can cause the oxidation of fats. Any of these can lead to diseases such as cancer, chronic disease and early aging. Antioxidants prevent oxidation by interfering with these reactions. To simplify: polyphenols and antioxidants are good guys.

Tea Promotes Longevity (The drink is declared to be most wholesome, preserving in perfect health until extreme old age.)

If we look back at Garraway's circular, we see the first claim Garraway made about tea was that it promoted longevity. He was absolutely right. Drinking a lot of tea can actually slow the aging process. In fact, doctors at the Saitama Cancer Center in Japan studied survival rates of patients with cancer and compared them to their green tea consumption. The amazing results showed that men who drank more than 10 cups per day died 4.5 years later than the men who drank fewer than 3 cups daily. The statistics on women were even better! (Woman lived 6.5 years longer if they drank 10 cups daily as opposed to fewer than 3 cups daily.) These are impressive numbers.

There have been many studies done on tea and prostate cancer, tea and ovarian cancer, and tea and breast cancer.

Green tea might help prevent the spread of prostate cancer as the polyphenols attack and interrupt the growth process of the cancer, preventing it from spreading and metastasizing. Other studies have shown that it might actually prevent it from starting in the first place. Black tea is known to have these properties as well, but seems to have a slower effect. It's not known how much tea one much ingest to incite a response such as this, but preventing or slowing prostate cancer might be seen as a way to help promote lusty behavior!

According to Dr. Mitchell Gaynor on Tea Lovers.com, another study conducted in December 2005 in Stockholm, Sweden, showed a relationship between the number of cups of tea a middle-aged woman drinks and her risk for ovarian cancer. Medical records for more than 60,000 women between the ages of 40 and 76 who had participated in a survey on cancer were studied. After 15 years, the study group showed that the women who drank tea had a 46 percent lower risk of ovarian cancer when they drank two or more cups per day.

In Japan, women with stage I, II, and III breast cancer were also studied for the effects of green tea consumption. Premenopausal women who drank more green tea than other premenopausal women had lower numbers of lympnode metastases. And postmenopausal women who drank green tea had better prognoses on their cancers than women who did not. In a follow-up study seven years later, it was found that the woman with stage I and II cancers who drank five or more cups of green tea daily had a 50 percent decreased recurrence rate than those who drank four cups or less.

What else did Garraway claim? Let's go through the list.

1. Tea and Flu (It helpeth the headache, giddiness and heaviness...It is good for colds, dropsys, and scurvys, if properly infused, purging the body by sweat and urine, and expelleth infection...It prevents and cures agues, surfets, and fevers, by infusing a fit quantity of the leaf, thereby provoking a most gentle vomit and breathing of the pores, and hath been given with wonderful success.)

The most important polyphenols in green tea are called catechins. Catechins are believed to prevent the carcinogenic effects of cancer-promoting chemicals and other diseases. Catechins found in green tea leaves include epigallocatechin gallate (EGCg), and epigallocatechin

(EGC). A recent study on catechins' effect on influenza showed that EGCG and ECG were found to be potent inhibitors of the virus that causes flu symptoms. Especially if you gargle with it! To sum up: It looks like Garraway might have scored another one! (In addition to working against flu, there is evidence that green tea can inhibit other viruses as well, such as herpes simplex and polio.) EGCg also strengthens the immune system by promoting growth of T-cells and B-cells, which fight disease. Go, tea!

> *"Drinking a daily cup of tea will surely starve the apothecary."*
>
> —Chinese Proverb

2. Organ Health (It removeth the obstructions of the spleen; It is very good against the stone and gravel, cleaning the kidneys and ureters, being drank with virgin's honey, instead of sugar...It removeth lassitude,

and cleanseth and purifieth acrid humours, and a
hot liver.)

Does tea promote organ health? There is evidence
that tea helps prevent heart disease. Flavanoids are
compounds found in tea that have been linked with
heart health. Specifically, according to the American
Heart Association, in several studies, people with a low
flavanoid intake had a higher death rate due to heart
disease than did those who drank flavanoids in 5 or 6
cups of tea per day. Drinking large amounts of flavanoids, however, was seen to have an adverse effect on
other areas of health, such as gastrointestinal and aller-
gies. Another study, done in Israel, found that people
who drank black tea had lower cholesterol than a contr
group who didn't consume black tea. While these studie
do not provide conclusive evidence that drinking black,
green or oolong tea reduces heart disease, significant ris
reduction does appear likely. One study of 4807 Dutch
men and women who drank 1.6 cups of black tea daily

had a much lower risk of heart attack than those who did not (68 percent lower). Some critical thinking might be useful when analyzing data like this, however. People who tend to drink tea might be the kind of people who have other life factors that also make them less of a risk of heart disease as well. There might be other factors at play here, but there does appear to be evidence to suggest that tea is heart healthy.

In another study, released by the Third International Scientific Symposium on Tea and Human Health, of 81,093 women ages 40 to 65 years old, it was found that one cup of tea consumed every day lowered the risk of getting kidney stones by 8 percent. As tea stimulates the production and flow of urine, tea might promote better kidney function.

3. Tea and Respiratory Health (It taketh away the difficulty of breathing, opening obstructions.)

There is currently no research that supports a

connection between green, black, and oolong tea and one's respiratory health other than the relief a hot cup of tea provides when one is stuffy and sick with a cold. Tea has been known to soothe throats and help clear nasal passages as the steam travels through the system. However, it is known that the EGCg in tea does help protect against respiratory infections.

4. Tea and Digestive Health (It is good against crudities, strengthening the weakness of the ventricle, or stomach, causing good appetite and digestion, and particularly for men of corpulent body, and such as are great eaters of flesh.)

Research has also been done on the link between tea and weight loss. The caffeine in tea might actually increase the number of calories burned. In one study, people who drank 3 to 4 cups of green tea daily had a significant loss in body fat when compared to people drinking a placebo. Of course, if you consider tea as a beverage choice while trying to lose weight, stay away from the milk, honey, and sugars, which add calories. Whether or not tea actually burns calories, it's a calorie-free (when consumed alone choice that is certainly a healthier choice than sodas or sweetened teas.

5. Tea and Caffeine (It vanquisheth heavy dreams, easeth the frame, and strengtheneth the memory. It overcometh superfluous sleep, and prevents sleepiness in general; a draught of the infusion being taken, so that without trouble, whole nights may be spent in study, without hurt to the body, in that it moderately healeth and bindeth the mouth of the stomach.)

Who doesn't remember using caffeine to stay up all night studying for a test? But is this a health benefit? Is caffeine good for us?

As we've seen, tea has less caffeine than coffee. It also has less caffeine than colas. As a stimulant, tea increases the action of the central nervous system, which results in an increase in heartbeat, respiration, metabolic rate, and the production of stomach acid and urine. Too much caffeine and you can become irritable and lose sleep. However, for generally healthy adults, who limit their caffeine to 3 to 4 six-ounce cups per day, adverse effects should be minimal. Each individual's reaction to caffeine can be different, however, so you should monitor your own symptoms and adjust accordingly. Many adults have trouble sleeping if they ingest any caffeine at all after early afternoon, while others can drink caffeine right before bed and drift off to sleep with little problem.

Some studies have linked caffeine intake to osteoporosis in woman. But one study actually found that that tea actually helped protect women against hip fractures, which as most of us know, can be very serious in older people. People who get enough calcium should be fine drinking tea with caffeine, and might benefit from it.

There have been warnings about caffeine consumption and fibrocystic changes in breast tissue (lumpy breasts). However, there is no conclusive evidence of a definite link between caffeine consumption and fibrocystic breasts.

By and large, it would seem that the health benefits of tea outweigh the possible adverse effects. And most likely, the worst side effect you'll find from too much tea is insomnia. But, as in all things, moderation is key!

So, what did Garraway miss? (And we must say here: Those citizens of the seventeenth century seemed unexpectedly informed!) Is there any other good news about tea? In addition to cancer prevention, improved cardiovascular health and possible reduced risk of stroke (due to health blood vessels and lower cholesterol), possible weight loss (due to extra burning of calories), increased metabolic rate, the retardation of the aging process (go, green tea!) and the boosting our of immune systems, tea has a few more tricks up its sleeves.

• Tea is good for your smile: The American Dental Association reports that the tannins and fluorides in tea actually prevent tooth decay, the buildup of plaque and bad breath. A cup a day might keep the dentist away!

• Tea might be good for your joints: Study results reported in the Proceedings of the National Academy of Sciences show that polyphenols found in green tea may effectively reduce the occurrence and severity of rheumatoid arthritis.

• Tea might reduce cancers of the throat: In 1994, the Journal of the National Cancer Institute published the results of a study indicating that green tea consumption reduced the risk of esophageal cancer in Chinese men and women by nearly sixty percent.

• Green tea might make you beautiful: Recent research has shown that green tea might have even more antioxidant properties than vitamins A, C, and E. Beauty products featuring green tea have been flooding the market, including moisturizers, sunscreens, even green tea perfumes!

Herbal teas have many different health benefits that we won't cover here. You can find many books dedicated to the health benefits of all the different herbs, and some wonderful recipes for home-brewed herbal teas.

Tea, whether green, black or oolong is not a miracle in a cup. It is a delicious, comforting, and social experience that can make your life a little more enjoyable. Tea is not a substitute for vitamins, minerals, vegetables, and doctors' visits. But the evidence is compelling that there are many positive reasons to put on the tea kettle and sit down at the table with a nice hot cup of your favorite tea.

"Tea! Thou soft, thou sober, sage, and venerable liquid...thou female tongue-running, smile-smoothing, heart-opening, wind-tippling cordial, to whose glorious insipidity I owe the happiest moments of my life, let me fall prostrate."

—Colley Cibber, *Lady's Last Stake*

QUIZ: DR. TEA—TEST YOUR TEA HEALTH KNOWLEDGE

Answers to this quiz can be found on page 473.

1. The following components of tea make it a healthful beverage choice:
a. Polyphenols
b. Tannins
c. Antioxidants
d. Flavanoids
e. All of the above

2. True or False: Tea might promote weight loss.

3. True or False: Gargling with green tea might prevent an incidence of flu.

4. Tea has been shown to prevent:
a. Hair loss

b. Menstrual cramps

c. Hunger pains

d. Headaches

e. Tooth decay

5. True or False: Drinking large amounts of tea might prevent gastrointestinal distress.

6. Tea might help prevent the onset of the following:

a. Rheumatoid arthritis

b. Prostate cancer

c. Multiple sclerosis

d. a and b

e. b and c

7. One possible adverse effect of drinking too much tea is _____.

8. True or False: Green tea is a good substitute for an annual visit to your doctor.

CHAPTER FIVE:

Tea Leaf Reading

A quick look at any online bookstore and you'll find thousands of books on fortune telling and psychic phenomenon. It is quite clear that seeing into the future is as popular now as it was at the turn of the nineteenth century, when psychic fairs were extremely popular. Tea leaf reading might conjure up images of gypsy women and dark tents, so you might be surprised to find out that this ancient practice is as alive as it ever was all over the world. References to tea leaf reading can be found in books (think of Harry Potter and the Prisoner of Azkaban), on television, and in movies. It's as popular today as it was when it sprang up in ancient cultures in Asia and Greece. Did you know, for example, that tea leaf readers were found in Europe as soon as tea was introduced and that by Victorian times it had become a popular parlor game? Some people even read coffee grounds! But tea lovers like us would, of course, do no such thing. Tea reading is for the truly enlightened.

Most of the material in this chapter is from Cicely
Kent's *How to Read Your Fate in a Teacup*, a terrific book
written in 1922 with a wealth of information. Some of
the material has been updated to reflect changes in the
times.

Tea leaf reading is also known as *tasseography*,
Tassa, the root, is the Arabic word for cup.

Preparation

Tea leaf reading does not require a large investment in
materials. But you will need the following:

- A wide, shallow, plain cup with a white interior
- A plain, unpatterned saucer (optional)
- A good quality tea free of twigs and other debris

A wide, shallow cup is the best kind to use for tea
leaf divination—white if possible. A narrow cup adds
to the tea reader's difficulties, as the leaves cannot be

lainly seen. Small cups, too, are objectionable for the
ame reason, and a fluted cup is even worse. Make sure
our cup has a plain, even surface, with no pattern of
ny kind on the inside, as patterns have a tendency to
onfuse the symbols. Of course, the exterior of the cup
an be as decorative as you please. Do not use cracked
nd chipped cups: The readings are not as strong with
amaged goods.

Indian tea and the cheaper mixtures, which tend to
ontain much more tea debris, are of no use for reading
fortune, as they cannot form into pictures and sym-
ols that can easily be distinguished. The twigs and
ust muddy the readings. Psychic Diane Ahlquist, in
er book *The Complete Idiot's Guide to Fortune Telling*,
lls us that black teas are said to be superior when it
omes to tea leaf readings. She recommends trying
eemum, which is considered "the finest of all the
hinese varieties." She also recommends using
arjeeling, or green teas, or oolong teas because they
e full-bodied. Of course, the tea must be loose. Please

do not use tea found in tea bags: this tea is too fine. And stay away from powdered teas as well.

Of course, you will want to prepare beyond gathering your materials. Getting ready for a tea reading involves picking the right cup, choosing a suitable tea and brewing the tea itself. Each action should be done meditatively, focusing carefully on what it is you are doing and what your concerns are for this particular reading. What is it that you want to know?

Brew your tea and let it steep at least three minutes before attempting a reading. Now enjoy your cuppa!

MUGS ARE NOT SUITABLE FOR TEA LEAF READING: You must use a wide and shallow cup. Ideally a porcelain one. If a cup with a white interior is not available, another very light color could be suitable as well, but you must be able to clearly see the leaves through the color. Under no circumstances should you do a tea leaf reading in a plastic or foam cup.

You should leave about a teaspoonful of tea at the bottom of the cup after you drink your tea. Take the cup in your left and turn it three times from the left with a quick swing. Then very gently, slowly, and with care, turn it upside down over the saucer, leaving it there for a minute, so that all the moisture may drain away.

Some readers insist on silence so they can concentrate their minds during this turning of the cup while the cards are being shuffled; others prefer the mind to be as free as possible from any definite thought or desire, simply allowing it to be blank or float from image to image.

The turning of the cup before inverting it over the saucer is equivalent to the shuffling of the cards. It is as a direct result of those few seconds turning that the pictures and signs are created, the subconscious mind directing the hand holding the cup. The simple ritual that follows is all that is necessary to those consulting the tea leaves.

The cup to be read is held by the reader (the seer) and turned about as necessary, so that the symbols may be read without disturbing them. This is important, but no disturbance will take place if the moisture has been properly drained away. The handle of the cup represents the sitter (the person whose tea leaves you are reading), also the home, or, if the sitter be away from home the present abode.

It is necessary to have a starting point in the cup for the purpose of indicating events approaching near to, or far from, the sitter. The leaves near the rim denote things that may be expected to occur quickly; those directly beneath the handle indicate present and immediate happenings; those on the sides of the cup suggest more distant events; while those at the bottom deal with the far distant future.

This method of fixing the time, coupled with intuition, renders it possible to give a sitter some idea as to when an event may be expected; but if you have no intuitive sense of time, you'd be wise to leave this element out of your reading.

Once you have turned the cup and drained the moisture as indicated above, the tea leaves will be found distributed at the sides and the bottom of the cup.

An alternate means of reading is to use the saucer as well. There must be a definite point to represent the sitter, however, and for this reason the saucer is usually rejected. There is no handle on the saucer to use as a point of reference. There is also the objection that it is more difficult to manipulate the saucer during the turning process. Nevertheless, it is found to give excellent results, and, if the cup is bare of events, it is useful to be able to find information in the saucer. You can always try to take a reading of the cup first, and if this doesn't work out well, move on to the saucer.

Here is a suggestion for determining a position to mark the position of the sitter (the point of origin) while doing a saucer reading: Take the center of the saucer for this purpose. The circle around it represents the home, or if the sitter is away from home, the present abode, and also events near at hand. The more distant circle indicates those things which are not to be expected for some time. The outer circle and rim suggest events as yet in the far distant future.

When the saucer is used as an additional means of seeking knowledge of coming events after the symbols in the cup have been exhausted, it will often be found that this secondary divination confirms or enlarges upon that which you already foretold in the cup.

Once you have drained the liquid and tea leaves drained from the cup into the saucer, the saucer should be turned by the sitter three times with the same swirling motion that was used for the cup, and the excess moisture carefully poured away.

The saucer should be held inverted for a few seconds, otherwise when it is placed upright, all of the remaining moisture will disturb the tea leaves. The symbols are read in exactly the same way as in the cup, the only difference being the positions representing the consultant, the home, and the indications of time as explained above.

Reading the Cup

At first sight the interior of the cup will appear to have the leaves scattered about haphazardly, with no arrangement; just a jumble of tea leaves and nothing more. In reality they have come into their positions and have taken on the shapes of the symbols they represent, by the guidance of the subconscious mind directing the hand in the turning of the cup.

At first the various shapes and the meanings to be attached to them will be puzzling to beginners. A good deal of practice is necessary before the tea leaf symbols can be accurately interpreted at a glance. That, however, will come later, and in time it will be as easy as reading a book.

If you wish to be a proficient reader, you will need to regularly practice your interpretation of the shapes and positions of the leaves. Take a cup and follow the simple instructions for the turning and draining of it, and then carefully study the result.

It might be helpful to make a rough drawing of the leaves as they appear in each of your readings. This way you can make notes on the readings and refer to them as practice readings, strengthening your abilities as you continue to read.

Don't be discouraged if at your first few readings you have difficulty making out any symbols in your reading. Certainly nothing will be discerned if you are anxious or nervous. Keep a calm, open mind, and don't hurry: You need a serene and open mind to make a clear reading every time.

However, please be aware that some

readings are just more difficult than others and symbols can present themselves clearly on some days while being harder to read on others.

The gifts of imagination and intuition (by no means to be confused with making things up) are great assets in discerning the symbols, which can appear in an endless array shapes and variety. The reader has to find —in the forms of the tea leaves— a resemblance, to natural objects. For instance, you might see the shape or suggestion of a flower, a bird, a mushroom, a tree, and so forth. Figures of human beings and animals will frequently be seen, as will squares, triangles, circles, and also the line of fate.

These signs may be large or small, and the importance of them must be judged by their relative size and position. Suppose, for example, that a small cross appears at the bottom of the cup and it is the only one to be seen, the reader would most likely predict that an annoying small delay can be expected. However, the

delay will not take place in the present as the cross
appears at the bottom of the cup. An alphabetical list of
symbols is given later in this chapter to help you figure
out what each symbol means (see, for example, CROSS
on page 289).

Stems, isolated leaves, or small groups of leaves
sometimes form a letter of the alphabet, sometimes a
number. These letters and numbers have meanings that
must be looked for in connection with other noticeable
signs. For instance, if an initial "M" appears, and near
to it a small square or oblong leaf, and both are near
the rim of the cup, you could predict that a letter will
be coming very soon from someone whose name begins
with an "M." If the initial appears near the bottom of
the cup it shows that the letter will not be coming for
some time.

If there is a space at the bottom of the cup devoid of
tea leaves, it shows water, and that, in all probability,
the letter is coming from abroad. If the symbol of the

letter comes very near to a bird flying, it shows an e-mail. If the bird is flying toward the consultant (the handle), the e-mail has been received. The news in it is to be judged by other signs in the cup. If the bird is flying away from the handle, the e-mail is sent by the sitter. A single bird flying always indicates speedy news.

In a cup with various ominous signs, such as a serpent, an owl, or many crosses, the news coming is not likely to be pleasant. In a cup without bad signs, it can safely be said that the news is good.

As a general rule, large letters indicate places, while smaller ones give the names of people. Thus a large letter "E" could stand for Edinburgh and a smaller "E" for Edwards, for instance. To all rules, of course, come the occasional exceptions and this principle holds true with regard to the letters in the tea cup. It is said that these smaller letters always point to the first letter of the last name. Usually it is so but it can also, on occasion, point to the first letter of the first name, or even a pet name. It

is well to keep this possibility in mind; otherwise the
reader might give incorrect information to the sitter.

Sometimes numbers mean the date of a forthcoming
even. A "5" for instance, very near the brim of the cup,
or the handle (which indicates the sitter), would mean
5 days. A 5 appearing on the side of the cup would
mean 5 weeks, and if the 5 appears at the bottom of
the cup it could mean 5 months from the present time.

As dots around a symbol always indicate money in
some form or another, according to the character of the
symbol, a figure beside the dots would signify the
amount of money to be expected. If the symbol were
that of an inheritance with the figure "90" near, it
might mean that a windfall of $90 might be expected
sometime soon, so the sitter might feel the urge to buy
a lottery ticket!

Clearly defined symbols that stand out separately are
of more importance those that are difficult to make out.
Clusters of shapeless leaves represent clouds marring

the effect of an otherwise fortunate cup.

Journeys are shown by lines or dots formed by any tea dust and smaller leaves. The length and direction of the journey may be known by the extent of the line and, roughly speaking, the point of the compass to which it leads. The handle represents south. If the line of dots ascends sharply to the brim of the cup, a journey to a hilly or mountainous place will be taken.

If the reader is doing a reading at the sitter's home, and the dots form a line from the handle all round the cup and back to the handle, it signifies a journey for a visit and the subsequent return. If the line were to stop before reaching the handle again, with an appearance of a house where the line ends, a change of residence might safely be predicted. A wavy line shows indecision as to arrangements. Crosses upon the line indicate that there will be an annoying delay in connection with the journey. Large flat leaves some distance apart along the line stand for important stations to be passed through.

For some sitters there might be very little of interest to be read in their cup. There are no events, just trivial details. It is therefore difficult to find anything that could be considered as a future occurrence—everything appears to take place in the present and there is nothing to read aside from the daily routine. The reader, in these cases, will just do his or her best to make the reading as interesting and engaging as possible.

A confusing and muddied tea leaf pattern, without any definite symbols, is useless for the purpose of divination, beyond giving an indication of the state of the sitter's mind: The vague reading is an indication of an undecided and clouded mind. Perhaps the sitter is disturbed about something in his or her life, or undecided about an action or decision to be made. This state of mind might obscure everything and the result is the unclear reading. You can relay your findings to the sitter and promise a future reading when things might be different.

Some people use the tea cup simply for the purpose of asking a definite question, such as: "Will I be healthy for a long a time?" Make sure you ask the sitter if he or she is hoping for a specific question to be answered. Then clear your mind and focus on the matter at hand. You can then look for any signs that will be answer the question posed, and you can ignore any other symbols, which might point you off in another direction entirely.

For Fun or for Study?

The need for patience cannot be too strongly emphasized for those who are just beginning to learn the language of tea leaves. Some of the most interesting symbols can be very difficult to notice and if the reader is in a hurry they will be missed entirely.

Of course, you might not want to dedicate the kind of time you need to put in to learning the intricacies and subtleties of tea leaf symbols and interpretations. If you'd like to read teas for your own enjoyment and

interest, you can do more superficial reads, noting just
the chief features that present themselves, such as a
journey, a letter, a package or news of a wedding, and
pass on to the next cup. But a deeper effort and understanding will give you much more insight and information about your own life or the life of those for whom
you read. There is no doubt, however, that you will be
as equally fascinated by your own life and readings of
your future as you will be by the readings that you do
for others!

It is amazing how quickly converts are made to this
form of fortune-telling. You might find that your skeptical friends are the ones who clamor the loudest for
readings. People who have loudly protested the existence of psychic phenomena have been known to
quickly sit themselves in front of a tea leaf reader to see
what the leaves have to say. So try not to gloat too
loudly when this happens to you!

Hints for the Novice Reader

You may be feeling quite skeptical and doubtful yourself.   After all, how can you definitively tell a hat from
a table when you are reading leaves left over from
someone's cup of comfort? It won't be helpful to point
out that these objects are perfectly represented by the
leaves. That is of no practical satisfaction to the
doubter. The simple fact that each language has its
alphabet, its spelling, and its words, which must be
learned before there can be any reasonable understanding of it, seems the best reply. The more you read, the
more you believe. The more you read, the more you
see. It's that simple!

Symbolism is not an exact science. There are many
subtleties and gray areas when it comes to interpreting
tea leaves. Who can expect to master such a language
quickly? If you cannot accept the symbols in the tea
leaves on the authority of the past experience of those
you came before you (reaching over several centuries,

as we have pointed out) here is a recommendation for you: Undertake a careful study of your cups for, say, three months. Make notes of all signs that appear and beside these notes place the meanings of the symbols and the predictions you make.

At the end of this time, compare your notes with the actual outcome of your predictions. Your lack of faith in this process is sure to fall away when you see the results in black and white.

Consistency

It is important that as you learn this art you consistently attribute the same meanings to the symbols. Do not be tempted to change their interpretation for what may seem a more probable, or pleasant, prediction for your sitter. This will be a terrible mistake. Remember that you are dealing with conditions and events of the future: These events are outside the limited knowledge of the normal mind, whose power of vision is limited to physical sight. You are entering a new realms and consistently and diligence are of paramount importance.

Here's an example of what may happen if you randomly change the symbols from reading to reading. Even one occurrence can cause big trouble.

A friend comes to have her fortune read. You are aware that she is anxious to hear a hopeful report about someone she loves who is seriously ill. However, the tea leaf symbols are stubbornly showing an unfortunate outcome and display ominous signs of eminent grief. If you gloss over this fact completely, and predict a rapid recovery from the illness, what becomes of your client's faith in the power of foretelling the future? Certain it is that the symbols would be right in their verdict, and you would be wrong. And interfering in another's future is one of the most fundamental breaches of faith with divination of any kind. Any fortune teller must stick to the readings as she sees them and abstain from embellishment where certainly is in question. What would happen if you told your friend her loved one would recover spontaneously in order to give her short-term comfort? She might act on your words. She might miss an opportunity to spend last final, precious moments with someone she loves very much, or to make amends for a past transgression. Eventually, you will not be thanked for your efforts at minimizing another's grief. Trust the leaves and be as kind as possible if you must deliver some unhappy readings. It is obviously much more enjoyable to foretell happy events than it is to tell of impending doom. However, your responsibility as a tea leaf reader is to the readings and the craft. Your sitters want to hear what the leaves say, not what you have to say. The only alternative is to hold back information, which we'll cover below.

You will see the truth of the leaves when you come across negative readings. For you will look into your heart and know that you wouldn't wish such negatively or doom on anyone. The leaves don't lie, but people do.

Of course, even with a lot of practice, you may occasionally make mistakes when reading the symbols, but never deliberately give a wrong interpretation of them to please your sitter. Your business as a fortune teller is to give what you believe to be the unprejudiced translation of the symbols before you. So make every effort to be consistent with your interpretations and leave personal feelings out of the readings.

Witholding Information

If you do get a gloomy or disastrous reading for a sitter, how much information should you give out? Some readers are in favor of withholding information (but never giving false information), while others announce it frankly without modification. It seems impossible to lay down any hard and fast rule. There are so many things to be taken into account, and each case should be treated on its merits and according to its peculiar circumstances. Some sitters might worry themselves into the grave at the smallest mention of coming misfortune, others would be the better prepared to meet it by having been warned beforehand.

One rule can be safely made for guidance on this point: Do not minimize danger when a timely warning may avert an accident, or other misfortune, nor should symbols of ill omen be exaggerated. As you become proficient, you will find many meanings in the tea leaves in addition to those you can learn from this book. In fact, much will depend upon circumstances and your individual personality and temperament. These personally discovered meanings should be carefully noted and verified with events as they occur.

Fortune telling by tea leaf reading is by no means limited to personal information, by the way. Forthcoming public events are frequently revealed. This adds largely to the interest and usefulness of the divination. It is important to point this out to the sitter so that so that he or she may doesn't limit the desired outcome to purely personal matters. However, public information is more likely to show up in reading with people who have their tea leaves read on a more regular basis. For those rarely attend readings, private affairs alone will appear—probably without even a forecast of the weather for the next few days! One would think the opposite would hold (that people who had their tea leaves read on an infrequent basis would only hear impersonal, public information).

Writing in the Tea Leaves: Some Frequent Symbols

Sometimes, quite remarkably, you will actually see writing in the tea leaves. Obviously one of the great advantages of seeing actual written words is that they are very easy to decipher! There's no intuiting and interpreting what an actual written message might mean (most of the time!). The tea leaves can never be accused of being illegible. Occasionally the writing is actually very tiny, and would probably be passed over by those who read their cups in a superficial manner. To those who study them carefully, however, the future will be revealed to them.

No one would reasonably expect to find a speech from the President or an invitation to a tea party written for them in the tea leaves. But they certainly will find words.

Be forewarned the tea leaves might have some trouble spelling, so be open-minded and keep our judgments to yourself. The spelling errors are usually minor and shouldn't interfere with your understanding of the writing. It is a well-recognized rule that writing seen through a medium, whether it be tea leaves, or a dream, is of importance, and should always be regarded with utmost attention. Make every effort to be vigilant and careful not to miss such messages.

Certain figures and symbols occur so frequently that we'll emphasize their general significance by referring to them here, in addition to giving their meaning in the dictionary.

Among those that signify misfortune, or sorrow, are the following:

- Crosses
- Snakes
- Spades
- Pistols
- Guns
- Toads
- Cats

Joy and success are indicated by symbols such as:

- Crescent moons
- Clover
- Leaves
- Flowers
- Trees
- Anchors
- Fruit
- Circles
- Stars

Once you have learned the symbols and the combined symbols by heart, it will require only a little practice to interpret their meanings without hesitation. If you find difficulty in committing the dictionary to memory (unfortunately an essential for proficient reading of the cup), try writing down any meaning which may seem especially hard to remember, roughly drawing its symbol beside it. In this way the difficulty will soon be overcome.

CHAPTER SIX:

A Dictionary
Of Symbols

Tea leaf reading relies on your own ability to read the symbols and intuit meanings from them. There's a lot to be learned, but don't be overwhelmed. Just study the list of symbols below to familiarize yourself with the patterns of interpretation. Make every effort to eventually memorize this list. The language of symbolism is obviously not an exact science so bring your intuitive side to bear and trust your instinct. You are the tea leaf master; the manual of symbols is not. It's time to get in touch with your inner wisdom and unlock your intuitive self. And remember: Symbols are changing as the world changes. At one time, readers would speak of telegrams while today we might speak of e-mails. Years ago planes would never appear as symbols at all. So as the world changes, be open to new symbols in your readings. The only thing we know for sure is that everything changes!

There are few things more fascinating than self-discovery, and those who become students of divination by tea leaf reading will certainly discover much about themselves. Tea leaf reading is an adventure for those who aren't afraid of the unknown!

a

ABBEY—A sign of increasing wealth and comfort; you will gain much success in your life.

ACE OF CLUBS—This signifies good news through the mail.

ACE OF DIAMONDS—You will be gratified by a good present or sum of money.

ACE OF HEARTS—Shows affection and happiness in the home.

ACE OF SPADES—A large town or building.

ACORN—This is a symbol of health, strength and gain through industry, a sowing of which you will see the reaping, a short journey from which there may be great results; good fortune and ease are predicted by several acorns. Basically, an acorn is a symbol of success.

AIRCRAFT—If flying toward the sitter's position in the cup, hasty news or an unexpected journey; if stationary, it warns that you will have but little success in your life unless you come out of the rut into which you have fallen.

ALBATROSS—If seen with the sign of a ship or water it portends distress for those at sea; to sailors or to those associated with them it is an omen of sadness, meaning sorrow and sometimes death.

ALLIGATOR—This is a bad sign of personal danger and distress possibly caused by those nearest to you; it also shows much mental disturbance and worry; if very near consultant, a catastrophe is imminent.

ALMONDS—These denote festivities and social enjoyment, good and generous friends.

ALTAR—If with a figure near, sorrow and distress are foreshown.

ANCHOR—A pleasing symbol of good and loyal friends, constancy in love, and the realization of your wishes; an emblem of safety to a sailor. An indication your concerns and worries will soon go away.

ANEMONE—These flowers often indicate an event to be expected in the early autumn; the nature of it must be judged by other signs in the cup.

ANGEL—This is a symbol of good fortune in love, radiance, happiness, and peace.

ANGEL (FLYING)—A token of love and joy which are swiftly approaching you.

ANTLERS—An accident is predicted by this symbol.

ANVIL—Your strength and energy will bring you much success in new plans or enterprises.

APE—This animal points to the fact that you have a secret enemy; it denotes malicious and dangerous persons whose tongues are to be feared; it is also a sign of despondency, care, anxiety, and fraud.

APPLES—A pleasant sign of happiness, cheerful conditions, good health, and fortune in business.

APPLE TREES—These predict a happy event in the apple season.

APRON—Near consultant brings a new friend; at a distance new work or acquaintances.

ARCH—Things which you desire are developing in the wished-for direction; the arch is a sign of hope; your ambition may be gratified in a most unexpected manner. See also TRIUMPHAL ARCH.

ARK—This symbol assures you of security and of finding refuge in times of distress and turmoil.

ARM—If curved, it signifies love, protection, care and strength; stretched out, that a new influence will come into your life which will prove to be an endless source of joy and love.

ARMOR—A suit of armor foretells that you will be called upon to face difficulties and dangers and that you will come through them with courage. See KNIGHT IN ARMOR.

ARROW—Unpleasant news or a disagreeable letter from the direction in which it comes.

ARTICHOKE—This signifies sadness, disappointment and delay; sometimes a secret trouble is indicated by this symbol.

ARTIST—To see an artist at work, indicates association with those who study art; also a happy nature finding much joy and beauty in life.

ARTIST'S MAHL STICK—This implies an artistic temperament, a dislike of daily duties or irksome tasks, and a fretting under any routine; a lack of attention to detail is also a usual characteristic of this symbol.

ARUM LILY—This flower stands for dignity, expectancy, and calm; its fuller meanings must be judged by other symbols around it.

ASS—If its head is facing the sitter's position on the cup, a piece of good news or an event which has long been waited for is near; if its tail, then further patience is necessary, for there will be delay; if it gallops, it gives warning that if people allow themselves to become too boring their friends may reasonably be expected to avoid them.

ASTERS—These flowers indicate a smooth though possibly a somewhat monotonous life; they also show a settled state of mind and sound judgment; if seen in the form of a wreath a death is predicted.

AXE—This shows mastery and power to overcome difficulties; sometimes separation.

b

BABY—A naked baby near the sitter is a sign of sadness and disappointment caused by those who are nearest and dearest; to some it is a sign of money worries; a baby in arms means reconciliation.

BABY CARRIAGE—News of a birth.

BACON—Pieces of bacon signify good luck and profitable business.

BADGER—For a single woman or man, this symbol predicts a single life, but one of freedom, health and success; for the married, it implies regret that they did not remain unmarried.

BAGPIPES—This symbol gives warning of coming sorrow or much agitation and disturbance.

BALL—See FOOTBALL.

BALLET DANCE—This is a forecast of unsuccessful plans.

BALLOON—A symbol which indicates that much is attempted but little achieved; there is a passing enthusiasm for various experiments and new ideas, but the interest soon flags, and finally vanishes as the balloon in the clouds.

BANANAS—These promise gratification and the occurrence of those things which are most pleasing to you; also a prediction of much happiness and success in love affairs.

BANNER—This is a symbol of a prosperous life for a man and of a wealthy marriage for a woman.

BARBER—This signifies the approach of a new interest coming into your life, which will lead you to be most particular about your personal appearance.

BARREL—Festivity, possibly a picnic; several barrels, prosperity.

BARREL ORGAN—Melancholy and a distaste for present circumstances.

BASIN—This symbol stands for small ailments and minor worries; a broken basin, domestic annoyance.

BASKET—Domestic duties and family cares; if full, a present given or received.

BASKET OF FLOWERS—Happiness and contentment, fulfilled desires.

BASSOON—This musical instrument implies that your energy is apt to exceed your wit.

BAT— A love of sports and a strong desire for fair play in all matters.

BATH—This indicates grief or dismay.

BATS—An ill omen showing sickness and trouble in the home; with other signs, a prediction of death. A fruitless journey or task.

BAYONET—A sign to be feared; it shows danger of operation, wounds, and pain.

BEANS—These show quarrels and disputes with relations.

BEASTS—other than those mentioned already, beasts tell of misfortune to come.

BED—A visit, illness; or death, according to other symbols.

BEEF—A side of beef foretells coming financial worries.

BEEHIVE—This is a symbol of eloquence, mental capacity, and much energy in forming new schemes and carrying them through; also of attainment to power and honor.

BEES—These foretell success through your own ability, many friends and enjoyment of life to the full. See also BUMBLE BEE.

BEETLE—This signifies unrest, domestic tribulation, or disagreements; several beetles, that there is a risk of slander and abuse by those whom you regard as friends.

BEETS—This symbol indicates that someone will try to do you a bad turn, but it will fail in its object and rather turn out as a benefit.

BELL—Amazing news according to other signs in the

cup; several bells indicate a wedding. See also CANTER-BURY BELLS, DIVING BELL, HANDBELL.

BELLADONNA LILY—This flower is a sign of hope, love, happiness, and the leading of an upright and honorable life.

BELLOWS—These show an endeavor to make the best of a bad business.

BESOM—This gives a caution to avoid meddling in other people's affairs or you may find yourself regarded as an unpleasant busybody.

BIER—A symbol of death; if near consultant, a personal sorrow, otherwise of a less personal nature.

BILLIARD OR POOL TABLE—Pleasure followed by regret.

BIRD FEEDING YOUNG—After a time of patient waiting, your desires will be fulfilled.

BIRD OF PARADISE—Difficulties and trials are vanishing and a future of comfort and pleasure awaits you.

BIRD ON A PERCH—If near consultant, news resulting in pleasant plans; if at some distance, there is a doubt of the news being sent.

BIRDS—These are significant of happiness and joyful tidings; a single bird flying means speedy news, e-mails; birds in a row on a branch or line show that there will be an annoying delay in receiving some wished-for news; birds in a circle denote cogitation followed by swift decision. Birds also tell of good news flying. See also CLAPPER FOR SCARING BIRDS and STUFFED BIRDS.

BIRDS IN CAGE—This implies that a variety of causes prevents you from obtaining your dearest wish; should the cage door be open, obstacles will shortly be removed and great happiness will be yours.

BIRD'S NEST—This signifies a happy discovery, leading to a fortunate enterprise brought about to a great extent by your own patience and ability; it is also a good omen of love, friends, and increase of fortune.

BISCUITS—These seen in various shapes and sizes foretell the occurrence of pleasant events.

BISHOP—A sign of benevolence, authority, and progress.

BLUEBELLS—These indicate that an event bringing you much satisfaction and pleasure may be expected to take place in the spring.

BOAR—This animal shows much energy, though not always in the right direction to bring you unqualified success; it is also a sign of obstacles in your path.

BOAT—Success in a new enterprise; seen with clouds, troubles and disappointment. See also FERRYBOAT.

BOMB—This foretells a personal disaster or news of an explosion and loss of life.

BONES—These are an indication of misfortune surmounted with courage.

BONNET—This implies that youth will be past before you have the best happiness of your life.

BOOK—An open book shows a desire for information and a mind ever on the alert to understand new theories and facts; a closed book is a sign of expectancy.

BOOKCASE—This is a pleasing symbol of coming success through study and perseverance.

BOOMERANG—This sign means news from Australia, or that some unexpected development will lead to your having a great interest in that country; with signs of travel, that you will make your home there.

BOOTS—These show fortunate business, a good income, and the gratification of your tastes and pleasures; boots of a curious shape foretell an unfortunate enterprise ending in failure.

BORDER—See FLOWER BORDER.

BOTTLE—A sign of happy days; several bottles indicate extravagant tastes; small bottles, illness.

BOUQUET—This is a most fortunate symbol of coming happiness, love, fulfilled hope, and marriage.

BOW—A sign of reunion after absence or estrangement.

BOW AND ARROW—This denotes that there is unpleasant talk of your personal affairs which may do you harm.

BOWER—Happiness in love is proclaimed by this symbol.

BOX—An open box foreshows a troubled love affair; a closed box, that you will find something which you had lost.

BOY—This symbol must be read in accordance with other signs in the cup.

BRACELET—A discovery made too late.

BRANCH—A large branch is a sign of much independence and of success in carrying out an undertaking; the larger it is the greater your success; a broken branch signifies an attempt to organize a project or new scheme which will end in failure.

BREAD—A loaf of bread is a sign of the commonplace and of monotony; several loaves give warning against waste and extravagance; loaves of bread with crossed swords above them predict mutiny and disaffection among those whom the world trusted.

BRICKS—These signify new plans and enterprises which will lead to prosperity.

BRIDE—This sign indicates a wedding, coming joy, or a rival in your affections, according to other symbols around it.

BRIDGE—An advantageous opportunity; a fortunate journey. See also SUSPENSION BRIDGE.

BRIDLE—This points to the fact that you greatly object to interference or authority, and that you will always be "top dog" with your friends.

BROOCH—This indicates that you are likely to make a discovery greatly to your advantage, and may in time turn it to good account in the development of a patent; a brooch with dots around it predicts a present.

BROOM—This signifies that there is need for you to be careful in the choice of your friends, and to avoid rushing into an intimacy which you might later have cause to regret.

BUBBLES—See CHILD BLOWING SOAP BUBBLES.

BUCKLES—These foretell that some important arrangement of much personal advantage will fall through in an unforeseen manner, causing disappointment and dismay.

BUFFALO—A most unexpected and unusual happening, possibly causing agitation and uncertainty as to the best way to proceed.

BUGLE—This shows a desire for admiration and notice from all whom you meet; it also implies that it is high time to move yourself and become more energetic and industrious.

BUILDING—A sign of removal.

BULL—An ill omen of misfortune, attacks of pain, or of slander by some enemy; if it gallops with tail up, personal danger or illness of someone dear to you.

BUMBLE BEE—This shows a cheerful disposition, making the best of everyone and everything, easily gratified tastes and pleasures; many friends and social success; with other signs, travel is indicated.

BUNS—These signify social amusements and duties, also that you usually take a cheerful view of things even in troublesome circumstances.

BUOY—This is a symbol of hope; you have a good friend in all types of weather.

BUSH—Invitations and social enjoyments.

BUTTER—This signifies good fortune and success, the comforts of life, and a desire for the best of everything.

BUTTERFLY—Passing pleasure, power of attraction, many admirers, and flirtations; to the lover it speaks of inconstancy.

BUTTONHOOK—An exchange between friends, successfully organized plans, and a propitious meeting.

BUTTONS—If of various size and shape they mean that there will be many suggestions as to arrangements and new plans without anything definite being settled.

C

CAB—A sign of gloom, sadness and parting.

CABBAGE—This symbol points out that in spite of thrift and diligence, you will never be very rich.

CABINET—An unexpected and fortunate discovery, giving you much pleasure and satisfaction, possibly wealth and unthought-of prosperity.

CAGE—An empty cage shows that you expect to find all manner of amiable qualities in others which are entirely lacking in yourself. See also BIRDS IN CAGE.

CAKES—New friends, social success, invitations, and hospitality. See also WEDDING CAKE.

CALF—This signifies a need for gentleness and kindness to those with whom you associate.

CAMEL—A responsibility satisfactorily carried out; sometimes frustrated plans and endless delays; a camel laden means wealth from an unexpected source abroad.

CAMERA—This proclaims the fact that you are too fond of gathering new or clever ideas from others, with a view to passing them off as your own original thoughts whenever the opportunity arises.

CAMPANULAS—These flowers indicate that your hope is centered on one desire, and assure you of the certainty of obtaining your wish.

CANDLE—This is significant of trials, worries, or illness.

CANDLE EXTINGUISHER—An uncomfortable incident or episode which will put you out considerably.

CANDLESTICK—You have need to look at things from a wider point of view; to make the best of yourself you must cultivate perception.

CANNON—This denotes military and naval display and good fortune; with pleasant symbols around or near, such as a crown or star, promotion for someone dear to you in the service.

CANOE—This implies that a new friendship will eventually lead to a happy love affair.

CANOPY—This brings success through the help and interest of those who are socially or mentally your superiors.

CANTERBURY BELLS—These graceful flowers indicate that your happiness is to a great extent dependent upon others; if the figure of a woman appeared beside the flowers it will be through a woman that your best happiness comes, if a man were seen it will be a male to whom you must look for your chief joy in life.

CAP—This warns you to be cautious in your dealings with those of the opposite sex; it also points to the fact that those things which you desire to hide will become known. See also PEAKED CAP.

CAPSTAN—To those associated with the sea, this symbol gives warning of storms; to others, it predicts association with sailors.

CAR—Short journeys by road or rail, visits from friends; with other signs, some increase of fortune may be expected.

CARAFE—A pleasure which will depend entirely upon yourself is the meaning of this symbol.

CARAVAN—This signifies an independent nature, should a horse be harnessed to the caravan your ambitions will be fulfilled.

CARDS—See ACE OF CLUBS, ACE OF DIAMONDS, ACE OF HEARTS, ACE OF SPADES.

CARNATIONS—These sweet-scented flowers bring happiness, faithfulness, love, and good friends.

CARPENTER AT WORK—Necessary arrangement of your affairs is the meaning of this symbol.

CARRIAGE AND HORSES—This foretells that your affairs will prosper and that you may reasonably expect the comforts of life; a carriage without horses means that your riches will be transitory, leaving you in poverty; with other signs it denotes that you may be the victim of scandal.

CARRYING CHAIR—An omen of illness or accident.

CART—A symbol of fluctuation in fortune and of a tedious waiting for any settled improvement in financial affairs.

CARVING—Handsome carving is a sign of satisfaction and development.

CASTLE—You may expect fortune to smile upon you; a crumbling castle denotes disappointment and ill success in love and marriage.

CAT—This is an uncomfortable sign of trickery, meanness, and quarrels among relations, money matters probably being the disturbing cause; a cat jumping shows worries and difficulty.

CATERPILLAR—You are likely to be criticized unkindly by those who are envious of you, although you have no suspicion that these people are anything but friendly in their feeling towards you; there is slyness and deception, and it would be well to be on your guard or you may find unpleasant gossip has been spread about you.

CATHEDRAL—Prosperity, contentment, and happiness with those whom you love is the meaning of this symbol.

CATTLE—Profitable transactions.

CAULDRON—New opportunities which need careful consideration.

CAULIFLOWER—This signifies that even your best friends cannot describe you as constant or reliable.

CAVE—Unless you rouse yourself and use a little more push, you are likely to remain in obscurity all your life.

CELERY—A vigorous body and active mind which will preserve the energies of youth for a good old age.

CHAIN—An engagement or wedding; an entangled chain means a dilemma which will tax your ingenuity to the utmost; a long, thick chain indicates ties that you wish to undo; a broken one, trouble in store.

CHAIR—A small chair shows an arrival; a large one, deliberation over a new plan. See also CARRYING CHAIR, ROCKING CHAIR.

CHAMPAGNE GLASS—This is a symbol of good fortune and delight; to the sick, a good omen of recovery.

CHEESE—A large cheese denotes that you will benefit by the generosity of prosperous friends.

CHERRIES—A love affair, happiness, and health, are the meanings of this symbol.

CHESSMEN—These announce the fact that you will be troubled by matters which are difficult to adjust to your satisfaction, and you must expect a certain amount of anxiety and worry.

CHESTNUT TREE—An event of interest and importance may be expected in the spring.

CHESTNUTS—These show determination in carrying out a scheme which you think will benefit you.

CHICKEN—This shows new interests and pleasures; if roosting, domestic tribulation; if flying, troublesome matters.

CHILD—This is a sign that you will soon be making fresh plans or forming new projects; a child running means bad news or threatened danger; at play, tranquility and pleasure.

CHILD BLOWING SOAP BUBBLES—Occasions of sadness and joy in quick succession.

CHILD WITH DANCING-DOLL—The gratification of a wish through an entirely unexpected means.

CHILD WITH TAMBOURINE—Pleasure, lightheartedness, coming good news.

CHIMNEY—Unless you are cautious you will take a false step; a chimney with smoke to be seen means that you are content, and find pleasure in daily routine and a somewhat commonplace life.

CHINESE LANTERN—False security, the evidence of which will soon be brought to your notice.

CHISEL—A symbol of losses, dismay, and trouble.

CHRISTMAS TREE—This sign indicates that you may expect some special happiness at the Christmas season.

CHRYSANTHEMUMS—These beautiful flowers assure you of a long desired hope in connection with someone dear to you which will be realized in the autumn.

CHURCH—Courage, honor, and tranquility; a legacy.

CHURNING—This is a happy omen for good and successful results in all you undertake; you will be fortunate and will always take a turn in the right direction for your own happiness.

CIGAR—A wealthy friend or lover who will absorb all your thoughts; a broken cigar signifies a disagreeable incident or a quarrel.

CIRCLE—Money, presents, an engagement, faithful friends.

CLAW—This symbol foretells scandal or evil influence.

CLENCHED HAND—Indignation; disputes.

CLERGYMAN—Reconciliation in a long-standing feud.

CLOCK—A sign that you desire to hurry over the present and arrive at a time to which you are looking forward.

CLOUDS—These denote disappointment, failure of plans, and dismay.

CLOVER—A very lucky sign of coming good fortune.

CLOVES—This symbol proclaims the desire for appreciation and the wish to appear at your best on all occasions.

CLOWN—Your folly is apparent to everyone.

CLUBS—See GOLF CLUBS, ACE OF CLUBS.

COACH—If with horses, you may look forward to a time of ease and luxury; if without horses, it warns you against an act of folly or a harmful indiscretion.

COAL—Prosperity and good fellowship

COAL-SCOOP—This signifies domestic difficulties or annoyance at the turn things have taken.

COAT—Sadness caused through a parting; if the coat is ragged, distressing news; without sleeves, failure in a new undertaking.

COBBLER—This predicts a life of arduous and ill-paid work, poor health, and a struggle to make both ends meet.

COBRA—A warning of grave danger to you or yours.

COCK—A sign of forthcoming good news, of conquest and triumph.

COCKATOO—This bird indicates disturbance in the home and some vexation with friends.

COCONUT—Travel or interesting discoveries.

COFFEE POT—Dependence on creature comforts; slight indisposition.

COFFIN—A bad omen of coming bereavement; a coffin with a sword beside it shows death of a soldier; with a flag, that of a sailor; with snowdrops, death of a child or infant.

COLLAR—Perseverance in the face of obstacles will bring you a great reward.

COLLAR-STUD—A reminder of some tiresome or disagreeable little duty which you would fain forget.

COLUMBINE—These flowers foretell the renewal of a former friendship which is brought about by means of an unthought-of meeting.

COMB—You will find out that your confidence in someone was misplaced and this discovery will cause you much distress.

COMET—Favorable weather; unusual and interesting events; to lovers it is an   unfavorable omen of separation and blighted hope.

COMPASSES—This sign implies that you may expect to travel and to spend your life in interesting activities.

CONCERTINA—This symbol proclaims dilatory habits and feeble wit.

CONDUCTOR—See MUSIC CONDUCTOR.

CONVOLVULI—This flower shows feelings of sadness; love and hope which have lasted but a short time now leave only memories to which you cling.

CORKS—This sign shows the power of adapting yourself to your company, and of proving yourself useful in awkward situations.

CORKSCREW—This denotes that you will be vexed by inquisitive people who trouble you with questions.

CORMORANT—This bird is a symbol of agility, swift decisions, and the attainment of your ambition through the power of rapid thought and work.

CORN—This is a pleasant omen of wealth and success.

CORNUCOPIA—This symbol predicts great happiness and unqualified success.

COVER—See MEAT COVER.

COW—A calm, contented state of mind, peaceful and prosperous days.

COWSLIPS—A sign of joy; to the married it foretells a birth.

CRAB—Strife, family disagreements, an enemy.

CRADLE—A birth; a broken cradle, sorrow or anxiety about a child.

CRANE—Heavy burdens and anxiety.

CRESTS—These are often to be seen and must to some extent be read in connection with other signs in the cup; large crests indicate news of, or communications with, those in positions of authority; small crests, interesting family developments.

CRINOLINE—This predicts that unless you retrench in your expenditure, you will have but a pittance to spend upon your dress.

CROCUSES—These flowers are an emblem of joy, and of radiant happiness in love.

CROQUET-MALLET—A cheerful and patient disposition, always making the best of things, is the meaning of this symbol.

CROSS—You must expect to meet with hindrances and obstacles in the way of your desires; sorrow and

misfortune are also indicated by this symbol. See also
MALTESE CROSS.

CROSSED KEYS—A sign of authority, power and honor,
and an assurance of comfort and help in times of difficulty or doubt.

CROWN—Advancement and honor; the attainment of
your highest ambition.

CRUTCHES—This is an unpleasant sign of forthcoming
illness or accident which causes lameness for the time
being.

CUCUMBER—A new plan successfully carried out.

CUP—A large cup tells of a splendid opportunity coming your way which will ensure your future success; a
small cup means that a little anxiety is before you.

CUPBOARD—Disappointment in money affairs.

CURTAIN—This symbol proclaims that someone is hiding a matter from you which it would be to your advantage to learn; with other signs in the cup which are good you may conclude that the matter will be revealed to you shortly.

CYPRESS—This tree indicates that you bravely face a difficulty, and finally overcome it by your own endeavors.

d

DAFFODILS—A long-desired hope is about to come to pass, or a delightful holiday spent in the company of those most congenial to you.

DAGGER—If near and pointing towards consultant, it would be a bad sign of danger from wounds or an operation; if more distant, it shows a much less personal danger.

DAHLIAS—A sign of some important event which you may expect to take place in the autumn; it also denotes thrift and increase of fortune.

DAISIES—These imply that you have an attractive, child-like nature, finding happiness in simple pleasures; a circle of daisies means that you attract someone to you of the same nature as yourself who will become all the world to you.

DAMSONS—These denote complication of your affairs.

DANCE—See BALLET DANCE.

DANCER—A pleasant omen of coming pleasure and gratification, good news, happiness in love and friendship; it also means that you will receive an unexpected invitation; several figures dancing in happy abandonment foretell that your hopes and desires will be fulfilled, and that many changes will occur, all tending to your success and future happiness.

DANCING-DOLL—See CHILD WITH DANCING DOLL.
DANDELION—Unexpected news of the marriage of an old friend whom you had always supposed would never marry.

DATES—A pleasure which is unlikely to come up to your expectations is the meaning of this symbol.

DEER—An unfortunate indication that your ventures in new directions of work or business will end in failure; if running, a fruitless endeavor to undo your past mistakes; a dead deer, that you will be the innocent cause of distress to someone you love.

DESK—You will receive a letter which will upset you, or you will lose the friendship of someone with whom you have corresponded regularly for many years.

DEVIL—This symbol gives warning that reformation is needed, or you may find yourself so tightly in the grip of bad influence that it will be well-nigh impossible to extricate yourself.

DIAMONDS—See ACE OF DIAMONDS.

DISH—Anxiety in household matters; a broken dish is a foretaste of a greater loss.

DIVER—A great and unexpected piece of news which

will lead to a fortunate discovery; to the lover, it reveals deception.

DIVING-BELL—This sign predicts that you may one day find yourself in danger on the sea or river.

DOG—This symbol has many meanings which must be read in accordance with the other symbols; in a general way this sign indicates adverse conditions, the thwarting of life's chances, unfortunate love affairs, family misfortune and money troubles; a large dog sometimes signifies protection and good friends; a small dog, vexation and impatience.

DOLL—A festivity at which you will endeavor to conceal your feelings of boredom under somewhat foolish hilarity. See also CHILD WITH DANCING DOLL, RAG DOLL.

DOLPHIN—A cheerful and optimistic character, pleasure on the sea or river.

DOOR—This indicates a visitor from beyond the grave. Also means knowledge of the past.

DOVES—These birds give a personal message of happiness and an assurance of faithfulness in love, peaceful circumstances, high ideals, and progress; to those who are estranged this symbol proclaims reconciliation; to the sick or anxious, comfort and hope; to a business man, a fortunate omen of success.

DRAGON—Great and sudden changes about which there is an element of danger.

DRAGON-FLY—Tidings of unexpected occurrences, unlooked-for events, new and advantageous opportunities, sometimes new clothes or furniture.

DRUM—A hazardous enterprise or expedition is the meaning of this symbol.

DRUMMER—To a man, this foreshows popularity and a successful public career; to a woman, social success, a large following of friends and admirers, and power of gaining her own ends.

DUCK—A sign of a taste for speculation; if more than one duck, success in work and enterprise, profitable undertakings.

DUMB BELL—A chance meeting which will lead to the making of a new friend.

DUSTPAN AND BRUSH—You will be certain to hear of domestic tribulation amongst your friends or relatives; if this symbol appears in your cup with other signs of vexation, it would indicate personal domestic annoyance.

e

EAGLE—This predicts that you may expect most beneficial changes, the realization of a long-cherished hope, and possibly an inheritance of wealth from an unexpected source; a flying eagle shows the coming of wealth and honor after a change of residence; with a vulture, death of a monarch; a dead eagle, public loss and mourning.

EAGLE'S NEST—An eagle on its nest foretells association with those in places of authority and honor; it also denotes a life of wealth and ease.

EAR—A large ear shows that you will be shocked by hearing of some scandal or abuse; a normal ear means that you will receive some interesting and pleasant piece of news or valuable information.

EAR-RINGS—To a man, this symbol proclaims the displeasure of one of the opposite sex; to a woman, the humiliation of unrequited affection.

EARWIG—A sign of uncomfortable discoveries in the home, troubles with domestics, deceit and prying.

EASEL—A sign of marriage to widows and maids; to the married, increase of worldly goods; this symbol must be read in connection with other indications in the cup.

EELS—This is an unpleasant symbol meaning malicious tongues and treacherous friends, also gossip over money matters.

EGG-CUP—A sign of an escape from a threatened disaster.

EGGS—New plans and ideas, or a birth.

ELEPHANT—A sign of power, travel, promotion, happiness and stability in love and friendship.

ELF—This symbol should put you on your guard or you may be the victim of an unpleasant practical joke.

ELM TREE—A good omen of prosperity and coming happiness.

EMU—Lack of caution will not be one of your failings.

ENGINE—Journeys, trouble on the railway, strikes, accident, and hasty news are the meanings of this symbol.

ENSIGN—See FLAG.

ENVELOPE—Good news will be coming your way.

ESCAPE—See FIRE ESCAPE.

EXTINGUISHER—See CANDLE EXTINGUISHER.

EYE—This signifies penetration and the solving of difficulties; it also shows depth of character and love.

EYEGLASSES—You will make a beneficial discovery through surprising means.

f

FACES—Several of these denote an invitation to a party or wedding; ugly faces mean disturbances or bad news; pretty faces, pleasure and love; two faces upon one head, looking diverse ways, indicate that you may hear yourself accused of deception and falseness, or that these things may be practiced upon you; a bearded face, health and strength, but an indolent nature, which is a source of vexation to those around you.

FALCON—This bird warns you to be on your guard, for you have an enemy.

FAN—Love of admiration, frivolity, pleasure with the opposite sex.

FATE—This is indicated by a straight thin line of tea leaves which ascends towards the consultant; what may be expected of fate must be judged by the line itself and other signs in the cup.

FEATHERS—Large feathers signify achievement and prosperity; to authors, literary success; small feathers denote something of which you are afraid, but which you will meet with courage.

FEET—You will be called upon to take a decisive step in some matter which may lead up to an eventful change in your life.

FENCE—This means that there is but a step between you and success.

FENDER—You will constantly come in contact with someone to whom you feel a strong antipathy.

FERNS—Dignity, peace, and steadfast love are the meanings of this symbol.

FERRET—Jealousy and enmity are likely to cause you distress.

FERRY-BOAT—This symbol implies that difficulties will be smoothed away for you by the aid of good and useful friends.

FIELD MARSHAL'S HAT—To a soldier, or those who are associated with them, this is a sign of coming promotion, triumph, and of the attainment to honor.

FIGS—These indicate joy and abundance of the good things of this world; to those in business it is an omen of success and prosperity.

FIGUREHEAD OF A SHIP—A good omen for your future Welfare; this symbol predicts that you will be enabled to steer your course through smooth waters.

FIGURES—See NUMBERS, HUMAN FIGURES, RUNNING FIGURES.

FINGER—This usually indicates a special need for attention to be paid to adjoining symbols.

FIRE-ENGINE—An evidence of a serious fire of which you will hear or from which you will suffer; this must be judged by other indications in the cup.

FIRE-ESCAPE—An urgent warning to take all precautions against fire.

FIREPLACE—Your chief interests in life will probably lie in your home; small duties, simple pleasures, and a circle of friends.

FISH—News from abroad; with other signs of movement, emigration; a starfish is a sign of good luck.

FLAG—Danger, rebellion, and war are the meanings of this symbol.

FLEUR-DE-LYS—At the top of the cup, health and happiness. At the bottom of the cup, anger and strife.

FLOWER-BORDER—That for which you have long hoped and waited is about to come to pass.

FLOWERS—Many pleasant meanings may be given to this symbol, good fortune, happiness, love, marriage, and a large circle of admiring friends, being among them. See also BASKET OF FLOWERS, FOXGLOVES, LILY, FORGET-ME-NOT.

FLY—This signifies small vexations and annoyances, which will ruffle you considerably. See also BLUEBOTTLE FLY, DRAGON FLY.

FONT—News of a birth or an invitation to a christening party.

FOOT—This indicates a journey; a swollen foot, injury, or news of an accident to the foot.

FOOTBALL—Love of outdoor games, or a keen interest in the welfare of those who take part in them, is shown by this symbol.

FORGE—This implies a need for refinement and of reconstructing your ideas on many subjects.

FORGET-ME-NOT—This flower speaks of the attainment of a cherished hope, also that you will probably find your truest happiness in love and marriage.

FORK—This warns you against those who constantly flatter you; it would be well for you to be on your guard or you may one day awake to the fact that all this flattery was used as a tool to harm you.

FOUNTAIN—A most favorable omen foretelling happiness, success in love and marriage, prosperity in business, and good fortune in all you undertake; this symbol also points to an unexpected legacy.

FOX—This denotes that you may have an unsuspected enemy, possibly disloyal dependents; sometimes it means theft and trickery.

FROG—A change of residence; with other signs, new work or profession; with bad symbols around, unpleasant sights and stories.

FRUIT—A happy sign of forthcoming prosperity and general advancement.

g

GAITERS—Your chief interests will be in outdoor work and amusements; intellectual pursuits will not attract you; to clergy, or to those associated with them, gaiters indicate promotion.

GALLOWS—An omen of great distress and tragedy.

GARDEN ROLLER—An indication that things around you are liable to become somewhat unmanageable, and that you will need tact and strength to avoid being crushed by circumstances.

GARLAND—A sign of happiness, love and honor.

GARTERS—A contempt for feminine weakness is the meaning of this sign.

GATE—An excellent opportunity awaits you, perhaps the chance of a lifetime; massive high gates denote restriction, misery, or imprisonment.

GEESE—These indicate the arrival of unexpected and rather troublesome visitors.

GENTIAN—A memory, which is interwoven with sorrow and joy.

GERANIUM—This flower shows a strong will and determined character, contentment, and happiness; it also denotes two opposite natures who have a great bond of affection between them.

GIANT—There is, or will be, a serious obstacle in your path.

GIMLET—You will be unpleasantly reminded of a disagreeable fact.

GIRAFFE—You are apt to cause mischief through blundering and the making of incorrect statements.

GLADIOLI—These flowers indicate courage in the face of difficulty; hope and tenderness.

GLASSES—These show that you will entertain your friends on a lavish scale, and delight in hospitality, but will occasionally be confronted by difficulties in your arrangements. See also CHAMPAGNE GLASS, CUSTARD-GLASSES, EYEGLASSES, HAND GLASS.

GOAT—A new enterprise which has an element of risk about it; a goat is an unfortunate sign to sailors or to those connected with them.

GOLF CLUBS—These indicate a life so full of work that there is but little leisure for recreation.

GONDOLA—A visit to Italy, or another romantic location are the meanings of this sign.

GONG-AND-STICK—This symbol warns you to expect little else than the "trivial round and common task" for the present.

GOOSE—A venture needing much discussion and arrangement; plans are made only to be upset again, and unless you proceed with caution, you are likely to make a bad mistake.

GRAPES—These signify pleasure, abundance, fulfillment, and a life free from care.

GRASSHOPPERS—These insects give warning of a poor harvest season; for an old person the risk of chill leading to severe illness. Grasshoppers, according to psychic Diane Ahlquist, can also signify news of someone in the armed forces.

GRAVE—This symbol must be read in accordance with its position, also with reference to other signs in the cup; as a general rule, with gloomy signs it would bring a message of coming sorrow, or with cheerful symbols that a death would benefit the consultant.

GREYHOUND—This sign stands for energy and untiring activity, which will bring you unqualified success; it also denotes that you may expect favorable tidings of the result of a new enterprise.

GRINDSTONE—The aftermath of an indiscretion.

GUITAR—This symbol displays strong power of attraction for the opposite sex, also pleasant adventures ending in a happy love affair.

GUN—A very disquieting symbol, grave danger of a sudden calamity; with other bad signs, a violent death.

h

HAMMER—Troublesome little tasks which you are reluctant to undertake.

HAMMOCK—A mournful ending of something to which you had looked forward with delight.

HAM WITH FRILL—This denotes a nice invitation, hospitality, pleasure with your friends; also enjoyment followed by dismay; a ham without a frill means increasing fortune and success.

HAND—A sign of good fellowship, loyalty, and affection; it may also indicate a parting, a meeting or a bargain concluded; other signs around it must be noticed in order to read its special meaning. See also CLENCHED HAND.

HANDBELL—You would much like to startle the world by a wonderful discovery or amazing theory by which your name would be known for all time but you will need every possible good symbol to appear in the cup to give you any assurance of your ambition being gratified.

HANDCUFFS—Disgrace, imprisonment, misfortune, and dishonesty; this sign must be read in connection with others around it.

HANDGLASS—An illusion quickly dispelled is the meaning of this symbol.

HANDSCREEN—Even small demands sometimes necessitate great effort on the part of those to whom the demand is made.

HARE—The return of an absent friend after a long absence; if it is running, a journey is indicated; a dead hare foreshows money acquired through industry.

HAREBELL—Peace, a placid existence, and faithfulness in love are the meanings of this lovely little flower; with other signs you may expect news of a birth.

HARP—This is a sign of melancholy and predicts the possibility of a nervous breakdown.

HARRISSI LILY—These graceful flowers predict peace, joy, hope, and a wedding.

HARROW—This shows that much of your time will be given trying to make the lives of those around you smooth and happy, while you cheerfully spend your days in a somewhat monotonous manner.

HARVEST—A shock of corn is a somewhat sad emblem showing that you have sown that of which the reaping will be tears; it is also a warning of illness, especially to the aged.

HAT—A symbol of luck, presents, success in new work or enterprise; sometimes it foreshows the arrival of a visitor.

HAWK—This is an unfortunate symbol, as it denotes circumstances in which people and things seem to be working against you, placing you in awkward and embarrassing predicaments.

HEAD—A large head gives warning of family trouble or of serious illness; a very small head, waning ability or power; several heads, mental distress or derangement.

HEARSE—A sign of bereavement or of sad news of those who are bereaved.

HEART—A sign of coming happiness through the affections bringing joy into your life, or satisfaction through money, according to other signs near.

HEARTS—See ACE OF HEARTS.

HEATHER—A most fortunate sign of gratified wishes and of coming good luck; to lovers it is an assurance of much happiness.

HEDGE—This shows that through energy and perseverance you will surmount obstacles and carry all before you.

HEDGEHOG—You will be immensely surprised by hearing that someone whom you had always thought of as a confirmed bachelor is about to be married.

HEMLOCK—The shadows of your past life have an inconvenient habit of appearing at the most awkward moments.

HENS—Comfort and domestic felicity; a hen roosting shows domestic annoyance and money worries.

HIGHLANDER—This is a sign of sound business capacity and a plodding contriver in transactions.

HIVE—See BEEHIVE.

HOCKEY-STICK—Enjoyment for games and success in the playing of them.

HOE—This means that you will often have more to do than you can finish; each day things will occur needing your attention and increasing your work, but in spite of it you will have good health and happiness.

HOLLY—This indicates that something of importance may be expected to occur in the winter; unless gloomy signs appear in the cup, it may be assumed that the event will be a happy one.

HOLLYHOCK—You will have a friend, or lover, who will never disappoint you.

HONEYCOMB—Prosperous undertakings, honor and renown, and much which is delightful are foreshown by this symbol.

HOOP—You will find immense satisfaction in doing things that require energy even if they are of little importance.

HORNS—You have a powerful enemy, or at least someone who has feelings of animosity towards you, which may prove to be unpleasant in their result.

HORSE—Comforts, loyal friends, and pleasure; galloping horses mean that events are hurrying towards you over which you have no control, bringing many changes into your life. See also CARRIAGE AND HORSES.

HORSE-COLLAR—To those who own horses, or do business with them, this sign is a pleasant indication of success in some transaction; to others it would imply toil and a strenuous effort to keep things going.

HORSEMAN—See MOUNTED HORSEMAN.

HORSESHOE—An unexpected piece of good fortune, the achievement of your wish, and good luck in all you undertake; a double horseshoe hastens the arrival of your desires; a horseshoe reversed means an upset of plans causing much disappointment and vexation; a broken one denotes a dilemma, trials, or other such discomforts.

HOT-WATER BOTTLE—You will always find compensation in all trials and discomforts.

HOT-WATER CAN—Indisposition, irritability, annoyances.

HOURGLASS—A warning against delay in arrangements or thought-of plans; with other signs, the hourglass is a grave warning of peril through illness or accident.

HOUSE—A very successful transaction, a visit, a new home, security.

HUMAN FIGURES—These must be judged with regard to what they appear to be doing.

HYACINTH—This flower predicts love, joy, happiness, and gratified ambition.

i

ICEBERG—Caution should be undertaken in sharing your thoughts.

INDIAN—This symbol predicts news from India; the nature of the information, whether personal, public, pleasant, or the reverse, must be judged by other indications in the cup.

INITIALS—These frequently occur, and usually point to names of people from whom you may expect to hear shortly; or they may indicate places.

INSECT—An insect is an indication that your troubles are not as large as you think they are.

INKPOT—Expectancy.

IRIS—These flowers bring a message of hope and pleasure.

IRON—Small vexations or troubles which will quickly pass, is the meaning of this symbol.

IVORY—This foretells increased wealth and a well-merited reward for past industry.

IVY—Patience, understanding, steadfastness, and loyal friends are indicated by this sign.

j

JACKAL—You will run across a sly person or mischief maker.

JAM—Pots of jam caution you against extravagance and waste.

JELLY—This foreshows a time of pleasure and a time of pain.

JEWELRY—You may expect an increase of wealth, possibly good presents also.

JOCKEY—Successful dealing and good money enterprise; luck in racing and speculation.

JUDGE IN ROBES—Legal affairs, personal or otherwise according to other indications in the cup; this sign is often seen during a famous trial or when one is about to take place.

JUG—This shows good health and money making.

JUMP ROPE—Pleasure with children and popularity with them.

JUMPING FIGURE—Change which will be greatly to your advantage.

k

KANGAROO—You will receive an unlooked-for, interesting piece of news; it may indicate you have a rival.

KETTLE—This is a sign of illness; unless a human figure appears beside it, the illness is probably for the consultant; it is an omen of coming trouble.

KEY—Circumstances will improve, things will become easy, and your path will be made smooth; you may hope for success in whatever you have on hand; a key at some distance from the consultant denotes the need for the assistance of good and influential friends in times of difficulty. See also CROSSED KEYS.

KEYHOLE—This gives warning of a need for caution, for someone of whom you feel no suspicion is untrustworthy.

KINGFISHER—This beautiful bird signifies the return of someone for whom you have been longing; if flying, news of a surprising nature will speedily arrive.

KING ON HIS THRONE—Security and peace; it may also mean that you gain a high position through influential friends.

KITE—Vanishing pleasures and benefits, or scandal, are the meanings of this sign.

KNEELING FIGURE—A new enterprise or project; care should be taken to think it over well; do nothing rashly and seek reliable advice.

KNIFE—This is an unpleasant sign of quarrels, broken friendship, and tears.

KNIGHT IN ARMOR—This sign predicts good fortune, success in love, and loyalty to your friends.

KNIVES—These signify danger of wounds, attacks of pain, and dismay.

1

LADDER—This signifies advancement, influential friends, and the attainment of good fortune.

LAMB—An indication that you will be amazed by the success of a doubtful undertaking. See also PRANCING LAMB.

LAMP—This sign provides an assurance of good success in business. See also STREET LAMP.

LANTERN/LAMP—This shows that fear and doubt will mar your happiness and progress. See also CHINESE LANTERN.

LAUREL—This tree points to power, ability and health.

LEAVES—Prosperous results of your diligence, new friends, and satisfaction.

LEEK—This implies that you are anxious to come to the root of some matter of which at present you have only an inkling; with good signs around, you may expect to come to a satisfactory understanding.

LEG—This foretells a successful race with fortune.

LEG OF MUTTON—Depression and pecuniary worries is the meaning of this sign.

LEOPARD—This animal foreshows triumph over adverse circumstances or an evil report; two leopards, fortune and misfortune following each other in quick succession.

LETTERS—These are shown by oblong or square tea leaves, initials near give the name of the writer; with dots around they will contain money.

LETTUCE—This shows sleeplessness, possibly from the receiving of some perturbing news.

LIGHTHOUSE—A good sign of security and of light on your path whenever it is most needed; if crooked or broken, disaster at sea.

LIGHTNING—Forked lightning seen in a zigzag up the side of the cup shows bad weather conditions; if near the figure of a man or woman, it may possibly indicate death from lightning or electrical mechanism; if seen at the bottom of the cup and with a clear space indicating water, it would mean bad storms abroad causing damage and loss.

LILAC—This is an emblem of radiant happiness; joys shared with another, with whom there is perfect oneness of purpose and love.

LILY-OF-THE-VALLEY—A fortunate omen of realization, love, and marriage. See also ARUM LILY, BELLADONNA LILY, MADONNA LILY, HARRISSI LILY, WATER LILY.

LIMPETS—These denote that you want to wrest from others some valuable secret which they possess, but without success; limpets are a sign of good luck to fishermen and promise a big haul of fish.

LINES OF DOTS—These indicate journeys and their probable length and direction; to be read in connection with other signs of movement; wavy lines mean tiresome journeys or difficulties likely to be encountered; if the lines ascend sharply to the brim of the cup, a journey to a hilly country will be taken.

LION—One of the most fortunate symbols indicating high hopes and excellent prospects, association with distinguished persons, honor, and fame.

LIZARD—This suggests treachery and the probability of a plot being laid against you by false and deceitful friends.

LOBSTER—A pleasant event, or a good present, is shown by this symbol.

LOCK—Something is blocking you, or there is a great burden weighing on you.

LOCK AND KEY—You are warned against the loss of something which you value.

LOOKING-GLASS—This implies a desire to know the truth, even if it be unpleasant to you.

LUTE—This is a sign of a secret sadness of which those around you know nothing; to musicians, a good omen of success.

LYNX—To the married a bad omen of estrangement, possibly divorce; to others it denotes treachery or episodes of a painful nature.

m

MACARONI—This proclaims the sad fact that you must try to make pennies do the work of a dollar.

MACE—Promotion, a position of authority and achievement.

MACHINE—See AUTOMATIC MACHINE.

MADONNA LILY—This flower means perfection and peace, and the assurance of love and truth.

MAGNET—You will be drawn by an irresistible attraction towards someone for whom you will eventually feel more dislike than affection.

MAGNIFYING GLASS—You are given to such exaggeration that it amounts to untruthfulness.

MAGNOLIA—This tree brings calm and peaceful conditions after a time of unrest.

MAILBOX—Important or specially interesting correspondence is the meaning of this sign.

MAILMAN—Important and profitable news.

MALLET—You will arrive at a wise conclusion in a difficult matter. See also CROQUET MALLET.

MALTESE CROSS—You will emerge from one source of vexation or trouble only to fall into another.

MAN—You may expect a visitor.

MAN CARRYING A BURDEN—An unhappy marriage or an unfortunate love affair.

MAN CARRYING MACE—This points to personal promotion or the advancement of someone dear to you.

MAN SPEAKING FROM A PLATFORM—Public news or developments, which will specially interest or concern you.

MARS—This sign will often be seen, and indicates a courageous, energetic nature, fond of exploits and freedom, and shows a capacity for strenuous work; a fortunate symbol for a soldier.

MASK—For a lover, this predicts that unpleasant facts will come to light, of which at present there is no suspicion or indication, leading to an abrupt ending of the love affair.

MASS OF LEAVES—Arrivals and departures about which there are little difficulties.

MAST—This symbol must be read in connection with the surrounding signs.

MASTIFF—This dog warns you of an unexpected emergency in which there is danger of your being overpowered by the arguments of those who are better informed.

MAY TREE—This signifies the receiving of a joyous message.

MEAT—A sign of financial worry.

MEAT COVER—An unpleasant emergency or discovery.

MEDAL—You will be rewarded for past industry by future prosperity.

MEDICINE BOTTLE—An unpleasant sign of illness.

MEDLAR—This tree predicts a condition of transient happiness.

MELON—This means gratification and good news, and the deriving of much pleasure from the appreciation of those whose good opinion is of value to you.

MERCURY—This planet is constantly seen in the tea leaves and is a symbol of ceaseless activity of striving to attain great things; it also indicates good business capacity.

MERMAID—To those associated with the sea, this is a warning of shipwreck or other peril.

MICE—Indicate danger of poverty by fraud or theft.

MILK-CANS—These show an agricultural enterprise that will be to your advantage.

MILK-CHURN—A good emblem of future comfort and increased happiness.

MILKING-STOOL—A new venture about which you will feel somewhat dubious but which with care will be carried out successfully.

MINE-SHAFT—This is a hopeful sign of coming peace after a time of discontent amongst miners, or a coal strike.

MIRROR—Prophetic dreams; a love of truth.

MISTLETOE—This signifies that a cherished hope is unlikely to be fulfilled, or at any rate it will only be after many months have passed, and when you have become weary of waiting.

MITRE—A prediction of honor and promotion for a clergyman.

MONK—Religious controversy and disturbances.

MONKEY—This is an unpleasant indication that ugly rumors and scandal will be spread about you or yours; sometimes public notoriety; with other signs, it foreshows grief and pain.

MONKEY-ON-ORGAN—Difficult circumstances and a hard struggle are the meanings of this sign.

MONKEY PUZZLE TREE—A task lies before you that you will find hard, but for which you will afterwards be rewarded by meeting with great success.

MONOGRAMS—These will often be found in the tea leaves and will indicate someone of much importance in your life, whose initials are shown by the monogram.

MONUMENT—Someone in whose career you are much interested will rise to fame.

MOON—A crescent moon denotes good news, fortune, and romance; for a man it predicts public recognition and honor.

MORTAR—A sign of gloom, illness, emergencies.

MOUNTAIN—This gives promise of the realization of a great ambition and of the influence of powerful friends; many mountains indicate obstructions and sometimes powerful enemies in your career.

MOUNTED HORSEMAN—A sign of good friends, luck, and advantageous offers.

MOUSE—This invariably indicates that there is need for a trap to be set; it also gives warning that domestic worries are to be expected.

MUFF—This implies caprice and ostentation.

MUG—This symbol predicts a merry meeting.

MUSHROOM—This predicts that you will take a small risk and achieve a great success; to lovers, it foreshows a quarrel and possibly a broken engagement.

MUSIC CONDUCTOR—A good sign to a musician; to others it suggests that enthusiasm and good spirits will carry them through life very happily.

MUTTON CHOP—Fruitless discussion or indisposition are the meanings of this sign. See also LEG OF MUTTON.

MYRTLE TREE—This speaks of affection and peace; a declaration of love, and a happy marriage.

n

NAIL—Toothache and painful dentistry are foreshown by this sign.

NAMES—To see the name of a person or place, signifies events occurring in connection with such person or place; if good symbols appear, pleasant happenings may be expected; if gloomy signs, then trouble will arise associated with the name seen.

NARCISSUS—This flower shows sentiment and coming joy; also that some new idea will unfold itself to you in the spring and will prove to be of much advantage to you.

NECKLACE—A good present or money; a broken necklace shows that you will break a bond which you have grown to feel is unendurable.

NEEDLES—These denote mischief and deceit; sometimes disappointment in love.

NEPTUNE—This planetary symbol indicates a condition of chaos.

NEST—See BIRD'S NEST, EAGLE'S NEST.

NET—Toil or anxiety followed by amazing achievement and good fortune.

NOSE—A large nose denotes dissipation; a crooked one shows a wayward and untrustworthy character; a long, thin nose implies that you change your ideas on various subjects and alter your mode of life in accordance with your new ideas.

NOSEGAY—See BOUQUET.

NOTICE-BOARD—Your attention will be called to some fact which it will be to your advantage to learn.

NUMBERS—These are frequently found in the tea leaves, and must be read in conjunction with surrounding symbols. If the consultant has a lucky number, and this appears with good signs, it promises much success. An unlucky number with gloomy signs predicts misfortune. A journey with a five near obviously points out that it will be taken in five days, or weeks, and so on.

NUN—This is a sign that you will probably remain unmarried through your own choice; to the married it implies unjust suspicion.

NURSE—A nurse in uniform usually foretells illness for yourself or for someone dear to you.

NUT-CRACKERS—This portends that you will strive to solve a difficult problem, the result of which is of much importance to you.

NUTS—Gratified ambition and wealth are indicated by nuts.

O

OAK TREE—This is a good omen of wealth, strength, and attainment of cherished hopes; for a lover, it predicts happiness and prosperity in marriage.

OAR—Sport; amusements; a broken oar denotes recklessness for which you will pay dearly; for a lover or husband, this means affliction.

OCTOPUS—You are in danger and do not have all the information you need.

OIL-CAN—Work and worry are foretold by this sign.

ONIONS—You may expect that something which you supposed was a secret will be discovered, possibly through treacherous friends.

OPERA-GLASSES—You are in danger of losing the confidence of your friends because of your inquisitive questions.

ORCHIDS—These give a pleasing assurance of coming good fortune and a life of ease and wealth.

ORGAN—This must be read in connection with other signs around it; sometimes it means a wedding, death, or realized ambition; to a musician, it is a good omen of achievement. See also BARREL ORGAN.

OSTRICH—This symbol points to achievement in creative work; if running, you may look for startling news and rumors of public upheavals.

OTTER—You must expect to receive a disagreeable shock through some unpleasant spite on the part of those of whom you have always thought well, and regarded as loyal and affectionate friends.

OVERCOAT—You may expect to have changes in your life and become of much importance.

OWL—A bad omen of illness, misfortune, and poverty; if flying, you will receive tidings of grief; to lovers this bird is a symbol of bad news or unpleasant rumors; to those who are contemplating new work or enterprise the owl should be regarded as a warning to proceed with caution.

OX—An ox in his stall implies hospitality, domestic peace and abundance.

OYSTERS—These are a sign of enjoyment and expensive tastes, also that you will appreciate the pleasures of life more in your later years than in your youthful days.

p

PADLOCK—An open padlock means a surprise; a closed one, a need for precaution.

PAGODA—Foreign travels.

PAIL—You will be called upon to undertake a variety of things that you dislike.

PAILS ON YOKE—In the future you may hope for compensation for past trials and weariness.

PALACE—This portends good fortune and favors.

PALETTE—A hopeful sign of success to an artist or to those associated with one; to others, it suggests a need for deliberation and advice before embarking upon a new work or enterprise.

PALM TREE—This is a symbol of honor, fame, and victory; increase of wealth, love, and marriage.

PAMPAS GRASS—This is a sign that you will make a pathetic endeavor to find happiness in a life which is cast in a somewhat dreary lot.

PANSY—This flower is a symbol of understanding, modesty, and contentment; it is also a pleasant indication of faithful friends and happy days.

PANTHER—You may expect to be shocked at the treacherous behavior of a friend whom you had always regarded as honorable.

PARADISE—See BIRD OF PARADISE.

PARALLEL LINES—These predict well-thought-out and smoothly running plans.

PARCELS—These are shown by thick, square or round leaves.

PARROT—This is a sign of foreign travel, the making of many friends, and much mental energy; sometimes it gives a hint that there is an inclination to gossip and spread scandal.

PARSLEY—Small events will bring you satisfaction.

PEACOCK—A sign of the acquisition of property; a prosperous and happy marriage; with other signs, an unfortunate friendship.

PEAKED CAP—The arrival of a male visitor.

PEARS—Improved social condition and other advantages; this fruit brings success to a business man and to a woman a rich husband; one pear signifies a birth or new plans.

PEDESTRIAN—An important appointment or urgent business.

PELICAN—This bird is a symbol of loneliness, separation, and yearning for the unattainable; if it is flying you will receive news from those who are far away in isolated parts of the world.

PEN—See QUILL PEN.

PENGUIN—This strange bird indicates interesting news of expeditions and discoveries in the northern regions.

PENKNIFE—This is an unfortunate symbol of enmity, disloyalty, and jealousy.

PEONIES—You will probably be called upon to make a decision of much importance before another summer is past; broken peonies predict that you may possibly throw away your chance of happiness by coming to a wrong conclusion.

PEPPER-POT—This means vexation and unreasonable irritation which you will endeavor to conceal.

PESTLE—A sign of decisive measures; a remedy for a grievance or an ill.

PHEASANT—Good fortune; new friends; if flying, speedy and propitious news.

PIANO—This is a sign that you will make the most of your opportunities and will gain that for which you have aimed; to musicians, a sign of advancement.

PICKAXE—This sign proclaims labor troubles and strikes.

PIG—This assures you of gain and success in agricultural interests; it also denotes that you may expect a present of money or a legacy.

PIGEONS—These show reconciliation with someone dear to you from whom you have been estranged; if flying, important and pleasant news is on its way; if stationary, delay in the arrival of important news.

PILLAR—A symbol of strength, protection from danger, and of good and powerful friends; a broken pillar predicts sorrow and despair.

PINCERS—A painful experience; an injury; toothache.

PINCUSHION—Thrift, order, and a well-regulated household.

PINEAPPLE—A pleasing indication of wealth, rich friends, and good presents.

PINE TREES—Happiness followed by an aftermath of regret.

PIPE—A visit from a dear friend; several pipes foreshow news from a man who is much in your thoughts. See also MEERSCHAUM PIPE, PAN AND HIS PIPES.

PISTOL—An ominous warning of disaster; with other bad signs, of a violent death.

PITCHER—This shows an endeavor to relieve a rather dull and monotonous life, by throwing your energy into somewhat unnecessary work.

PITCHFORK—A sign that you are apt to stir up feud, and make peace and quiet impossible.

PLANE—A journey is in your future.

PLATE—For the present, you will merely jog along in an ordinary way.

PLAYING CARDS—See ACE OF CLUBS, ACE OF

DIAMONDS, ACE OF HEARTS, and ACE OF SPADES.
PLOW—You must expect to go through toil and frustration before you finally conquer your difficulties and achieve triumph.

PLUM PUDDING—This denotes festivity and cheerfulness.

PLUMS—These foretell a new development of plans.

POLAR BEAR—This sign means a journey to a cold climate.

POLICEMAN—This tells you to beware of theft and underhand practices; with other signs, it would indicate trouble probably caused by those with whom you are most closely associated.

POPE—Unexpected gain and future happines.

POPPY—This flower is significant of a pleasant occurrence in the early summer.

PORTER AND TRUCK—This indicates a pending journey or the arrival of a traveler.

POST—This signifies a formidable obstacle; if broken, that you will encounter a storm of opposition to your plan.

POT—See COFFEE POT.

POTATO—You will have need of patience in your daily life, and will sometimes be troubled by pecuniary difficulties.

PRANCING LAMB—This is a symbol of trouble that will have beneficial results and will lead to contentment and happiness.

PRAWNS—These bring pleasures, presents and satisfactory arrangements.

PRINCE OF WALES' PLUMES—This is a symbol of pleasant events, stirring topics and sometimes of personal honor and distinction.

PUDDING—See PLUM PUDDING.

PUFFIN—This bird denotes timidity and a desire for solitude; if flying, news from abroad.

PULPIT—A love of talking and a dislike to listening is the meaning of this symbol.

PUMP—Your own efforts will bring about a fortunate result.

PURSE—This cautions you against theft, or carelessness that may lead to losing money.

PYRAMIDS—These foreshow attainment to honor, fame and wealth.

q

QUEEN—A queen upon her throne indicates security, peace, and honor; sometimes the attainment to a high position through powerful friends.

QUESTION MARK—This shows doubt, indecision; if this sign were seen with a letter the doubt would be with regard to some correspondence; if with a journey, uncertainty about it; and so on.

QUILL PEN—This shows that you may expect, before long, to sign your maiden name for the last time in a marriage register; with other signs, a legal document.

r

RABBIT—An indication of illness for a child; a dead rabbit means domestic duties that will bore you, sometimes financial worry; several rabbits suggest that you must depend upon your own efforts for your amusements and must be content with simple ones; a rabbit on its hind legs predicts that a new plan or idea will bring you great success.

RAG DOLL—This implies a simplicity that sometimes verges on folly.

RAILWAY SIGNAL—This symbol may be seen at "danger" or "all clear." Its meaning must be read in accordance with other signs.

RAM—An unpleasant person whom you would do well to avoid is indicated by this sign.

RAKE—This implement denotes a persevering nature that should bring you a liberal measure of success in whatever you undertake; it also indicates luck in speculation.

RAT—Treachery and other impending troubles, are foreshown by this unpleasant symbol.

RAVEN—This bird is an omen of gloom and despondency, disappointment in love, separation, failure in work; it is also a symbol of death for the aged.

RAZOR—Quarrels, also a warning against interference in other people's affairs; to lovers this sign foretells disagreement and separation.

RED-HOT POKER—This flower suggests that you are likely to bring yourself within the range of unpleasant criticism by your flaunting manner.

REPTILE—This is a bad omen of coming misfortune, treachery, or illness.

RHINOCEROS—This animal denotes a risky proceeding into which you plunge without hesitation, although your friends and relations will try to persuade you to give up your scheme, but your indifference to the opinion of others prevents any chance of their being successful.

RIDER—This brings good news from overseas of business and financial affairs.

RIFLE—Strife and calamity are shown by this sign.

RING—With dots around, a contract or a business transaction; with the figures of a man and woman, an engagement or wedding is foretold.

RIVER—A sign of trouble and perplexity, sometimes illness and bereavement.

ROBIN—A symbol of much good fortune, loyal friends, and happiness in love.

ROBOT—This signifies a lack of initiative and consequent failure in arriving at any great achievement.

ROCKET—This foretells joy and gladness at some event about to happen.

ROCKING CHAIR—This indicates contemplation of a new idea or scheme about which you are somewhat doubtful.

ROCKING HORSE—Happy associations will be renewed; pleasure with children.

ROCKS—These prepare you for alarms and agitation, but if good signs appear, you will eventually find a smooth path through your fife.

ROLLER—See GARDEN ROLLER.

ROLLING PIN—This is an indication that you will be capable of smoothing out your difficulties and will usually find an easy path in which to tread.

ROSE—A token of good fortune, joy, and love.

ROSEMARY—Memories of the past will mar your future.

RUNNING FIGURES—You may expect an emergency in which you will need to have all your wits about you; sometimes this signifies urgent messages.

S

SACK—This predicts an unlooked for event which will turn out to be most fortunate.

SADDLE—The successful solving of a troublesome matter is the meaning of this sign.

SAILOR—You may expect news from overseas of an interesting nature.

SALMON JUMPING IN A POOL—This is a fortunate sign of propitious news that will mean a great deal to you.

SANDWICH MAN—After a time of irksome tasks and pecuniary worry, you will be rewarded by a time of ease and wealth.

SAUCEPAN—This is an indication that many troubles will befall you, and your courage will be tested in meeting them.

SAUSAGES—These show complaints or affliction.

SAW—Interference which will bring a good deal of trouble upon you, is signified by a saw.

SCAFFOLD—This signifies that you will enter into a rash speculation.

SCALES—This symbol stands for legal proceedings.

SCARECROW—This warns you to avoid interfering in the private affairs of others, or you may find that you will receive the cold shoulder from them.

SCEPTRE—This is a fortunate sign of distinction and honor.

SCISSORS—An unlucky sign of friction between friends; disputing and disagreeableness with married couples;

quarrels between lovers; trouble in business.

SCOOP—See COAL SCOOP.

SCREW—With a little ingenuity and perseverance, you will arrive at your goals.

SCREW-SPANNER—Troublesome affairs and vexations are before you.

SCUTTLE—See COAL SCUTTLE.

SCYTHE—This sign foreshows grief and pain.

SEAGULL—A sign of storms; if flying, news from abroad.

SEAL—An indication that a considerable amount of patience will be necessary before your hopes are realized, but eventually you will gain success and wealth.

SEALING-WAX—Theoretically you are wise, but you seldom bring your wisdom to bear on practical matters.

SEE-SAW—Unless you endeavor to become more decisive and reliable, you will lose any good opportunities that may come your way.

SEAWEED—This denotes a joy in the past of which only the memory remains.

SHAMROCK—A sign of good luck.

SHARK—An ominous sign of death.

SHAVING-BRUSH—This sign suggests that you are apt to turn molehills into mountains.

SHEEP—To landowners or those engaged in any agricultural pursuits sheep are an omen of success and prosperous dealing; to others this sign implies that they will receive assistance from unexpected quarters.

SHELL—Good luck from an unexpected source; with other signs, a visit to the seaside.

SHEPHERD—The appearance of this symbol warns you against taking unnecessary risks in all matters.

SHIP—News from distant lands; a successful journey; a voyage.

SHIRT—This sign is considered an omen of good fortune.

SHOES—These indicate speedy new arrangements that are likely to turn out extremely well.

SHRIMPING NET—Pleasures and amusements, unconventionality, and good spirits.

SHUTTERS—This sign proclaims the fact that there is need for secrecy, and that there may be things in your life of which you trust nothing will be known.

SICKLE—A sign that you will experience sorrow and pain through the callous behavior of someone you love.

SIGNPOST—This symbol must be read in conjunction with surrounding symbols; it usually emphasizes the importance of other signs; a broken signpost indicates, that you take a wrong turning in your life and afterwards have much cause to regret it.

SKELETON—This implies a feeling of disgust at some information which is told to you and which you are asked not to reveal.

SLEIGH—A spell of cold weather; an interesting event or piece of news to be expected in the winter.

SLUG—Petty annoyances; bad weather.

SNAIL—This is a sign of infidelity; several snails, that mischief is going on around you of which you are unaware.

SNAKE—This is an unpleasant sign of treachery, disloyalty, and hidden danger, sometimes caused by those whom you least suspect; if its head is raised, injury by the malice of a man is predicted; it is also an indication of misfortune and illness.

SNIPE—This bird signifies the discovery of a useful fact; if flying, hasty news of a great friend.

SNOWDROPS—These are a symbol of youth and innocence; this sign may point to some event affecting you and yours which will probably take place about February; if seen in a cross it would foreshow the death of an infant or young child.

SOAP—Cakes or blocks of soap predict temporary trouble in business.

SOAP BUBBLES—See CHILD BLOWING SOAP BUBBLES.

SOFA—This foreshows indisposition or a small illness, sometimes disturbed nights or emergencies.

SOLDIER—This signifies that you may count upon the loyalty and affection of your friends; sometimes it indicates that you may expect speedy news of a soldier.

SOLOMON'S SEAL—This plant is a symbol of understanding, devotion, and coming joy.

SOUP LADLE—It will be through the assistance of others that you will arrive at success.

SOUP TUREEN—To the mature, this symbol points to a return of good fortune; to the young, a small illness and loss of appetite.

SPADE—This means toil, care, unrest, disappointment, and failure. See ACE OF SPADES.

SPANNER—See SCREW SPANNER.

SPHINX—This denotes that your hopes will be set on things far beyond your reach, and that as nothing but the very best in life has any attraction for you, it is improbable that you will ever attain to complete happiness.

SPIDER—You may expect to receive an inheritance; with other signs, that you will be triumphant in disputed will or money settlements; several spiders foretell profitable transactions, sometimes heritage of much wealth.

SPUR—This symbol foretells that as the result of endurance and honest labor you will attain to honor.

SQUARE—This formed of dotted lines indicates perplexity and dismay, and endeavor to extricate yourself from an embarrassing situation.

SQUIRREL—This is a sign of contentment and cheerfulness; although you may never be rich you will be loved by those around you and, on the whole, will lead a happy life.

STAR—A lucky sign; if surrounded by dots, wealth and honor are foretold.

STEAMER—A voyage, news from overseas, interesting events, according to other signs.

STEEPLE—This denotes misfortune, bad luck; if it is crooked or bending it foreshows a coming disaster or crushing blow to your hope.

STEPS—Unaccustomed work which will fall to your lot as a result of the illness of someone with whom you work or associate.

STEREO—This usually portends vexation at being drawn into a somewhat disorderly and noisy pleasure.

STILTS—These show a desire to appear different in the eyes of your friends from that which you really are, and you will often fail in an effort to keep up this subterfuge.

STOCKS—These sweet scented flowers foretell an unexpected happiness with someone whom you have not seen for a long while.

STOCKINGS—A present received or given is the meaning of this symbol.

STONES—Little worries and vexations.

STOOL—A large stool is a symbol of honor; a small one signifies that your success in life will be meager.

STORK—In summer, this bird tells you to beware of robbery or fraud; in winter, prepare for bad weather and a great misfortune; a stork flying predicts that whilst you hesitate in coming to a decision, a profitable chance is lost, the news of which will speedily reach you.

STOVE—This symbol calls attention to the fact that trials and tribulations await you.

STRAW—A bundle of straw foretells gain through industry.

STRAWBERRIES—Pleasure and the gratification of your wishes are shown by this fruit.

STRAW HAT—Modesty and simple pleasures.

STREETLAMP—This is a sign of a foolish desire to draw attention to yourself.

STUD—See COLLAR STUD.

STUFFED BIRDS—A discovery that something upon which you had set your heart proves unsatisfying.

SUBMARINE—Swiftly arriving news or events; sometimes the disclosure of a secret which will be of much personal value to you.

SUN—This promises happiness, health, success in love, prosperity, and the beneficial discovery of secrets.

SUN BONNET—A sign of originality, personal charm and attraction, sometimes coquetry.

SUNDIAL—You are warned to take heed as to the way in which you spend your time.

SUNFLOWER—This flower proclaims learning and a satisfactory conclusion in matters which are most interesting to you; it also implies that you may reasonably expect a scheme to work out greatly to your advantage
.

SUSPENDERS—These show precaution.

SUSPENSION BRIDGE—A venture in which much is at stake but after a time of anxiety you arrive at final triumph.

SWALLOW—A journey with a happy result; if flying, joyful tidings from someone you love; if several swallows are flying, they indicate a journey to a warm climate under very pleasant conditions.

SWAN—This bird is significant of tribulation, troublesome conditions in the home, and sometimes of separation from those whom you love.

SWEEP—The performing of an urgent disagreeable business will shortly fall to your lot.

SWEET WILLIAM—This flower signifies that happiness in the past has tinged your future with sadness.

SWIMMING—A brave endeavor to overcome your fear of an undertaking which must be faced.

SWING-BOAT—By an act of folly, you forfeit the good opinion of someone with whom you most desire to be on terms of friendship.

SWORD—This is a sign of danger, sudden illness, or even death; it also is a sign of slander and dangerous gossip; to lovers it is a bad omen of quarrels; a sword in its sheath shows honor and glory for someone dear to you; a broken sword predicts the triumph of an enemy.

t

TABLE—This means suggestions and consultation; note the subject from the surrounding signs.

TAMBOURINE—A symbol of lighthearted gaiety that will follow a time of gloom or worry. See also CHILD WITH TAMBOURINE.

TEA COZY—To the unmarried, this is a sign that they will probably remain single; to the married, affection and comfort in the small things in life.

TEA CUP AND SAUCER—You may expect to hear something of much interest and pleasure in your "fortune."

TEAPOT—Expect a visitor: Friends are on their way.

TEETH—These call attention to the fact that probably a visit to the dentist is required.

TELEPHONE POST—Hasty news by telephone or fax.

TELEPHONE WIRES—You will translate important business by telephone or fax.

TELEPHONE—You will be put to considerable inconvenience through forgetfulness.

TELESCOPE—This predicts the probability of trouble with your eyesight.

TENNIS NET—This shows pleasures and social entertainments.

TENT—A symbol of travel.

THIMBLE—For a girl, this symbol implies that she will probably never marry; to the married, it predicts changes in the household.

THISTLE—This is a pleasant sign of strength, endurance, and affection; it also shows a desire to remove obstacles from the path of those who are having difficulties.

THRONE—An empty throne denotes public misfortune. See also KING ON THRONE.

THUMB—A large and powerful thumb foretells an opportunity in which you prove yourself superior to those who previously somewhat despised you.

TIGER—You will be placed in a perilous position possibly through the bad behavior or folly of those who should protect you.

TIMBER—Logs of timber are a sign of well-being and prosperity in your affairs.

TIN TACKS—An agreement about to be satisfactorily concluded.

TOAD—You may expect deceit and the discovery of disagreeable facts; this sign should caution you to be on your guard, for malicious talking causes much discomfort and may separate the best of friends.

TOADSTOOL—You are warned against making rash and unguarded statements, a bad habit of gossiping and encouraging scandal.

TOMATOES GROWING—An increase of worldly goods is foreshown by this sign.

TOMBSTONE—This sign must be judged in accordance with other symbols around it.

TONGS—A pair of fire tongs indicates anxiety and disturbance in the home.

TONGUE—This signifies that unless you amend you will make mischief by your indiscreet and unkind words.

TOOTH—One large tooth is a symbol of bereavement.

TOPIARY WORK—Trees and hedges cut into the forms of birds, animals, etc., are often to be seen in the tea leaves; this sign assures you of the fact that those things for which you must wait longest are those which will give most joy.

TORCH (FLAMING)—This is a hopeful symbol that some unexpected piece of good fortune will come to you; it also indicates the discovery of an undeveloped talent.

TORPEDO—Acts of violence, disaster, or distressing news are the meanings of this symbol.

TORTOISE—This means that you attempt that of which you have no knowledge.

TOWER—This predicts an advantageous opportunity through which you may rise to a good position in life.

TOYS—Pleasure with children.

TRAIN—Arrivals, removals, a journey.

TRAM—A roadway journey on business or pleasure.

TRAIN LINE—This is indicated by two thin, straight lines that run close together up the side of the cup.

TREES—Good health and a pleasing assurance of coming prosperity and happiness; if surrounded by dots an inheritance of property in the country is foreshown. See also CHESTNUT TREE, CHRISTMAS TREE, ELM TREE, OAK TREE, YEW TREE.

TRIANGLE—A fortunate meeting, good luck; sometimes an unexpected legacy.

TRIDENT—A hopeful sign of honor and promotion to those in the Navy.

TRIUMPHAL ARCH—This is a fortunate omen of your future honor and high position; a decorated arch foretells a wedding.

TROWEL—This gardening implement foretells good weather conditions; seen in the winter, it indicates unusual mildness. See also BRICKLAYER'S TROWEL.

TROUSERS—A pair of trousers predicts news of misfortune or sorrow for a man.

TRUE LOVER'S KNOT—This is a happy omen of faithfulness in love, and of enduring friendship.

TRUMPET—This denotes good fortune to a musician; to others, entertainment, large assemblies of people, public speaking, sometimes the setting on foot of new schemes.

TRUNK—Arrivals and departures.

TUB—You have evil to fear.

TULIPS—A symbol of radiance, health, and constancy in love and friendship.

TUNNEL—This suggests that you are likely to make a wrong decision in an important matter.

TURKEY—That you are in danger of making bad decisions is the meaning of this sign.

TURNIP—The discovery of secrets and domestic quarrels are indicated by this sign.

TURNPIKE—This implies that your reminiscences about the past are of more interest than your stories of the present.

TURNSTILE—This is a sign that you cleverly evade a disagreeable incident or unpleasant discussion without offending anyone.

TURTLE—This is significant of wealth and luxury.

TWINS—This is a symbol of sympathy and the perfection of happiness; with other signs, news of the birth of twins.

u

UGLY FACES—These show domestic quarrels or unpleasant news.

UMBRELLA—If it is open, bad weather and grumbling are predicted; closed, a bit of bad luck which may be avoided.

UNICORN—This is an indication of scandal.

URN—A sign of illness.

V

VAMPIRE—This brings a message of gloom and sorrow, or also means that you await the expected news of a death.

VAN—This sign denotes an interesting experiment in which you succeed.

VANITY BAG—A large circle of admiring friends, and much pleasure with them.

VASE—This sign brings you a promise of good health.

VEGETABLE MARROW—This means sad news or monetary losses through bad crops, either at home or abroad.

VEGETABLES—These indicate toil, followed by a time of leisure and affluent circumstances.

VEHICLES—Travel is in your future.

VENUS—This planet that is sometimes seen in the tea leaves, brings a message of peace or placidity.

VISE—A carpenter's vise signifies that you will need powerful assistance to extricate you from the mess in which you will find yourself through your actions.

VIOLETS—This is a symbol of high ideals and of the finding of happiness in its fullest sense; several violets assure you of coming joy; if in the form of a cross, death is predicted.

VIOLIN—A symbol of coming success to a musician, and of pleasure and entertainment to others.

VOLCANO—Watch those emotions! You or someone near you is about to explode.

VULTURE—This bird is a forewarning of evil and unrest in various quarters of the globe; it also means a powerful enemy, sometimes death; if it flies, tragedy, sorrow, and tears are predicted.

W

WADING BOOT—This is a warning to be cautious in swimming or boating, or you may meet with an accident; with other signs it denotes a home by the sea.

WAGON—This implies a fortunate outlook and changes for the better.

WALKING STICK—The arrival of a male visitor.

WALL—A thick, high wall denotes many difficulties in your life, and that much courage will be needed to overcome them.

WALLFLOWER—This sign indicates the serious consideration of a new plan.

WARMING PAN—This is a sign of comfort in small things and domestic peace.

WASPS—These insects are significant of distress caused by the sharp tongues of those around you.

WATER—This is usually recognized by a clear space entirely free from tea leaves at the bottom of the cup.

WATER LILY—This flower proclaims a declaration of love.

WEASEL—This animal shows cunning, and points to the sly behavior of someone with whom you associate, and of whom you feel no suspicion.

WEATHERVANE—This is a sign that you feel incapable of making up your mind definitely on any matter without first consulting each one with whom you come in contact, and in the end you settle upon an entirely different course of action.

WEDDING CAKE—This proclaims a speedy and prosperous marriage.

WHALE—A prediction of personal danger which may be averted if you are cautious.

WHEEL—This is symbolic of the wheel of fortune and predicts a prosperous career or an inheritance of wealth; a broken wheel predicts a bad disappointment in regard to an expected increase of income or a legacy.

WHEELBARROW—This sign foretells a visit to the country or a pleasant renewal of friendship with those who live there.

WHIP—To a woman this sign foretells vexation and trials in her marriage; for a man, it has much the same meaning, and severe disappointment will befall him.

WICKET GATE—A small incident leads up to an important future event.

WIDOW'S BONNET—This sign must be read in connection with other symbols; sometimes it predicts grief and mourning, or if dots are around it, that a sum of money or a legacy may be expected from a widow.

WINDMILL—A sign that you may hope to succeed in a doubtful enterprise.

WINDOW—An open window shows that you are regarded with favor by many; a closed one means embarrassment.

WINE CUP—Joy and realized ambition.

WINGS—You will get a message very soon.

WITCH ON BROOM—You will be reproved by some of your friends who consider that your interest in psychic matters is dangerous, but later on you will be able to prove to their satisfaction that no harm has come to it.

WITNESS BOX—With bad signs around it, this would point to a personal matter ending in a law court; otherwise, it denotes the taking place of a trial in which you will feel special interest.

WOLF—Beware of an avaricious and hard-hearted neighbor or friend.

WOMAN CARRYING A BURDEN—An unhappy marriage or unfortunate love affair.

WOMAN CARRYING A CHILD—This shows distress, sometimes illness of someone dear to you, or sadness through separation.

WOMAN HOLDING A MIRROR—Clairvoyance and prediction of the future are signified by this symbol.

WOMEN—With bad signs, several women mean scandal; otherwise, society.

WOOD—Much happiness with someone dear to you, a forthcoming wedding, or a fortunate and favorable event.

WOODPECKER—This bird brings pleasant news from those who live in the country.

WORMS—These warn you of coming misfortune, or of treachery, and evil by secret foes.

WREATH—This is a symbol of marriage, and of much happiness being in store for you.

y

YACHT—This is a favorable sign of increased wealth or happiness.

YEW TREE—You may expect to attain to a prominent position in life, and to receive a legacy from an aged relative or friend.

Z

ZEBRA—Something for which you have long waited is now within sight, but you are likely to be disappointed, for you will find that it was not worth waiting for after all.

SOME COMBINATIONS OF
SYMBOLS AND THEIR MEANING

ACE OF DIAMONDS, A CIRCLE—An engagement.

ACE OF DIAMONDS, A BUSH—A pleasant invitation.

ACE OF CLUBS, AN OBELISK—A good promotion.

ACE OF HEARTS, A TRAIN, A QUERY—Indecision about a removal.

ACE OF HEARTS, AN URN, A BED—Illness in the home.

ACE OF SPADES, BRICKS—An advantageous offer from a large town.

ARM, A MYRTLE TREE, BIRD ON A PERCH—New plans which bring about ameeting with someone who will become all the world to you.

ARUM LILY, BELLS, A CHURCH—A wedding.

ARUM LILY, A BAT, A BED, A WIDOW'S BONNET—
Death of a widow.

BACON, PAGODA—You will make your fortune abroad.

BANANA, A PEACOCK, ACE OF HEARTS, TREES—A
happy marriage to someone of wealth and property in
the country.

BED, AN ENGINE, LABURNUM TREE—A happy visit to
the country in the spring.

BESOM, UGLY FACES—You will make many enemies
by mischief-making.

BONNET, A BOUQUET—Marriage late in life.

BRIDE, A CRESCENT MOON, A SWALLOW—A
journey which leads to a romantic love affair.

BRIDE, PENKNIFE, AN OWL—Jealousy terminates an unhappy engagement.

CAB, A SQUARE, A CAP—A gloomy outlook brought about by one of the opposite sex.

CAMEL (LADEN), A SMALL "T," A COFFIN—An unexpected fortune through the death of someone abroad whose name begins with "T."

CHAIN (ENTANGLED), ONION—You will be placed in an embarrassing position by the discovery of a secret.

CHINESE LANTERN, A PAIR OF STILTS—Pride brings about a fall.

CLOVER, PLUMS, A BRIDGE—A new and excellent opportunity will come your way necessitating a journey.

DAFFODILS, THE SUN—A joyful occurrence in spring.

DOVES, A BOOK, A BEEHIVE—You will advance rapidly and become a well-known writer.

DUCK, A VEGETABLE MARROW—Rash investments.

EAGLE (FLYING), A STEAMER, A TENT, A LARGE "E"—A position of honor in Egypt.

EAR, A BEEHIVE, A TRUMPET—Fame as a public speaker.

FATE LINE, A SWORD IN ITS SHEATH, THE SIGN OF MARS, A CHAIN—A happy fate awaits you, and marriage to a soldier who will rise to the top of his profession.

FROG, A FISH, A SHIP, A LARGE "C"—Emigration to a country beginning with C.

GOAT, A RUNNING FIGURE, A LAMB—There need be no doubt as to the successful outcome of your venture.

GRASSHOPPERS, A SLEIGH, A WREATH OF ASTERS—Death of an elderly friend or relative in the winter.

KEY, A FLAMING TORCH—Some discovery or development of a patent leads to becoming famous.

KING ON HIS THRONE, AN EAGLE IN A CAGE, A MACE—An important public ceremony in which you take a part.

LADDER, RING, A MAN AND A WOMAN—Marriage will be the means of advancement and good fortune.

LADDER, A PALETTE—Attainment to a position of honor as an artist.

LADDER, THE SYMBOL OF MARS—A most fortunate career as a soldier.

LION, A LUTE—Rising to the top of the tree, as a musician, is assured by these symbols.

LION, A MAN SPEAKING FROM A PLATFORM—Great success in a public career and the attaining to an influential position.

LION, A MAN BESIDE A PESTLE AND MORTAR—Excellent prospects and fame as a doctor.

LIZARD, A PEAKED CAP—An expected visitor is not to be trusted.

MACE, A MALLET—Through wisdom and clear judgment you will rise to a position of authority.

MAN CARRYING A BURDEN, A PAIR OF SCISSORS, A MUSHROOM—Quarrels in an unhappy love affair ending in a broken engagement.

MAGNET, A MEAT COVER—An unpleasant discovery leads to the abrupt ending of an infatuation.

NAIL, A PAIR OF PINCERS—A visit to the dentist and the removal of a tooth.

NOTICE-BOARD, A LEEK, AN OPEN PADLOCK—In a surprising manner you will get the information for which you are seeking.

ONIONS, AN OTTER—Those in whom you trusted have betrayed your confidence and divulged a secret.

OWL, A PAIL—Loss of income will necessitate your undertaking distasteful work.

PAGODA, A PALM TREE, WATER—A voyage to a warm climate under very happy conditions.

PESTLE AND MORTAR, A WALKING STICK—Illness
and the arrival of the doctor.

PULPIT, OPERA GLASSES—Those who weary others by
undue curiosity will always remain in ignorance.

QUERY, A LETTER, INITIAL "B," A GRAVE STONE—
You will be consulted about the erecting of a headstone
on the grave of a relative or friend.

QUILL PEN, LILIES OF THE VALLEY, AN ORGAN—
Great happiness through marriage.

RABBIT, AN ARROW, A LARGE LETTER "L," A
DAGGER—News of severe illness and a probable operation for a child who lives in London.

RHINOCEROS, AN OVERCOAT, A STEAMER, A
LARGE LETTER "I"—The undertaking of a somewhat
hazardous enterprise necessitates a voyage to India;

through much will happen which will eventually lead to your becoming famous.

ROCKET, A PEAR, A SNOWDROP—News of a birth of which you may expect to hear in February.

ROCKING CHAIR, A PEDESTRIAN, A MUSHROOM—Deliberation over important matters brings you to the conclusion that a great venture, which may mean enormous gain, is worth a small risk, and success will await you.

SAILOR, A FLYING SWALLOW, A TRIDENT, A RING—Happy news of good promotion for a sailor and a proposal of marriage.

SCAFFOLD, LEG OF MUTTON—Gambling or speculation will bring you to poverty unless you pay heed to this warning.

SHARK, A PISTOL, A FLYING SEAGULL—News from abroad of a tragic death.

SNAKE, A RAM, A WOMAN, A WIDOW'S BONNET—Overwhelming evidence against some widow who is a dangerous enemy.

SOFA, A SLEIGH—A cold in the head or a chill.

SWORD, A RING, A MAN, A WOMAN, A TOAD—Separation of lovers brought about by slander

.

TABLE, A QUILL PEN, A CAT, A RING WITH DOTS AROUND—Legal business over money matters which leads to family quarrels.

THRONE, AN OSTRICH RUNNING, A FLYING SEAGULL, A FLAG—Serious news from abroad of disturbances and rebellion.

TRAIN LINES, A BUILDING WITH DOTS AROUND IT, A PURSE—You will take a roadway journey to a bank and are warned to beware of pickpockets.

URN, HOSPITAL NURSE, A MAN, A LARGE HEART— Serious illness affecting the heart is predicted for a man.

VEGETABLE MARROW, A STEAMER, A BROKEN PILLAR—Distressing news of misfortune for someone dear to you.

VIOLET, A WATER LILY, A ROBIN, A CRESCENT MOON, A RING—A romantic love affair which ends in a happy marriage taking place in the early spring.

WADING BOOT, THE SIGN OF NEPTUNE, SEVERAL PENGUINS, A MAST—News of a disaster in the North Sea.

WIDOW'S BONNET, A PIG, A DOTTED CIRCLE, THE FIGURE "100"—A small legacy of a hundred dollars may be expected from a widow.

WOODPECKER, TREES, A ROSE, A MAN—A prospective visit to the country in the summer, when you will meet with someone who will become very dear to you.

YEW TREE, AN OPEN PADLOCK, A WALLFLOWER, A PINEAPPLE—A new plan of life is made necessary as the result of an unexpected inheritance of much wealth.

AFTER THE READING

After a reading try to avoid talking too much about it as you might find yourself deviating from what actually occurred and is predicted through the readings, instead getting into your own wants and hopes for the sitter. Simply pack up your supplies (you may want to keep a decorative box for your various tea supplies) and put them aside and encourage the reader to end the reading. Keep your tea reading and your socializing divided to ensure the greatest accuracy in your fortune-telling.

If you follow the instructions in this book, you will most likely soon find yourself surrounded by people who want to have their tea leaves read. You'll be the most popular kid on the block! Through your interactions with others, you will soon find yourself gaining a wide and in-depth knowledge of human behavior and character. Like therapists, readers develop an understanding of human nature that goes far beyond the average person's comprehension.

Whether you read tea leaves for profession or just for amusement, you will find yourself wholly engaged with this wonderful new talent. And all you need is a cup of tea to be initiated into the fascinating art of reading the future in a tea-cup.

CHAPTER SEVEN:

A Word On Omens

The following information on omens was gathered from *Fortune Telling by Tea Leaves*, by "A Highland Seer." People have been seeing omens since at least Ancient Babylon. Omens were seen as either good or bad signs (depending on the interpretation). They foretold occurrences in the near or distant future. Omens could be seen in the appearance of animals, birds, fish, and reptiles, from outside or inside (entrails from sacrifices were not uncommon omens), and humans.

In India, where the records of the early ages of civilization go back hundreds of years, omens are considered of great importance. Later, in Greece, the home of the greatest and highest culture and civilization, omens were also regarded very seriously and, even to this day, omens are part of everyday culture.

Some ground for belief in some omens seems indisputable. Whether the result of experience, by the following of some particular event close upon the heels of

signs observed, or whether it has been an intuitive science in which provision has been used to afford an
interpretation, is not quite clear. It would be a mistake
to dismiss omens as mere superstition, wild guessing,
or abject credulity, as some try to do, with astrology
and alchemy also, and other occult sciences; the fact
remains that omens have, in numberless instances,
given good warnings. So pay attention closely and you
will expand your fortune telling dictionary of symbols
exponentially.

Many people will say that these are just coincidence.
But for those who believe, the universe is governed by
law. Things happen because they must, not because
they may. As they say, there are no coincidences. We
may not be able to see the steps and the connections.
But they are there all the same.

In years gone by, many signs were deduced from the
symptoms of sick men; the events or actions of a man's
life; dreams and visions; the appearance of a man's

shadow; from fire, flame, light, or smoke; the state and
condition of cities and their streets, of fields, marshes,
rivers, and lands. From the appearances of the stars
and planets, of eclipses, meteors, shooting stars, the
direction of winds, the form of clouds, thunder and
lightning and other weather incidents, they were able
to forecast happenings. A number of tablets are devoted
to these prophecies.

It is conceivable that many of these omens should
have found their way into Greece, and it is not unreasonable to believe that India may have derived her
knowledge of omens from Babylonia; or it may have
been the other way around. But it does seem clear that
the practice of seeing and interpreting omens spreads
all over the globe, to every area of the planet.

It would be difficult to attempt to classify omens.
Many books have been written on the subject and more
yet to be written of the beliefs of the various races. The
best that can be offered here is a selection from one or

other of the varied sources. In Greece, sneezing was a good omen and was considered a proof of the truth of what was said at the moment by the sneezer.

A tingling in the hand denoted the near handling of money, a ringing in the ears that news will soon be received. The number of sneezes then became a sign for more definite results. The hand which tingled, either right or left, indicated whether the money was to be paid or received. The particular ear affected was held to indicate good or evil news. Other involuntary movements of the body were also considered of prime importance.

Many omens are derived from the observation of various substances dropped into a bowl of water. In Babylon, oil was used. Today, in various countries, melted lead, wax, or the white of an egg, is used. The trade or occupation of a future husband, the luck for the year, and so on, are deduced from the shapes which result in the folk practices of modern Europe. Finns use stearine and melted lead, Magyars lead, Russians wax,

Danes lead and egg, and the northern counties of England egg, wax and oil.

Bird omens were the subject of very serious study in Greece. It has been thought that this was because in the early mythology of Greece some of their gods and goddesses were believed to have been birds. Birds, therefore, were particularly sacred, and their appearances and movements were of profound significance. The principal birds for signs were the raven, the crow, the heron, wren, dove, woodpecker, and kingfisher, and all the birds of prey, such as the hawk, eagle, or vulture, which the ancients classed together (W. R. Halliday, Greek Divination). Many curious instances, which were fulfilled, of bird omens are related in "The Other World," by Rev. F. Lee. A number of families have traditions about the appearance of a white bird in particular.

"In the ancient family of Ferrers, of Chartley Park, in Staffordshire, a herd of wild cattle is preserved. A tradition arose in the time of Henry III. that the birth of a parti-colored calf is a sure omen of death, within the same year, to a member of the Lord Ferrers family. By a noticeable coincidence, a calf of this description has been born whenever a death has happened of late years in this noble family" (Staffordshire Chronicle, July, 1835). The falling of a picture or a statue or bust of the individual is usually regarded as an evil omen. Many cases are cited where this has soon been followed by the death of the person.

It would be easy to multiply instances of this sort: of personal omen or warning. The history and traditions of our great families are saturated with it. The predictions and omens relating to certain well-known families, and others, reoccur at once; and from these it may be inferred that beneath the more popular beliefs there is enough fire and truth to justify the smoke that is produced, and to reward some of the faith that is placed in the modern dreambooks and the books of fate and the interpretations of omens.

OMENS

ACORN—Falling from the oak tree on anyone, is a sign of good fortune to the person it strikes.

BAT—To see one in daytime means a long journey.

BIRTHDAYS—

"Monday's child is fair of face,
Tuesday's child is full of grace,
Wednesday's child is full of woe,
Thursday's child has far to go,
Friday's child is loving and giving,
Saturday's child works hard for its living;
But a child that's born on the Sabbath-day
Is handsome and wise and loving and gay."

BUTTERFLY—In your room means great pleasure and success, but you must not catch it, or the luck will change.

CANDLE—A spark on the wick of a candle means a letter for the one who first sees it. A big glow like a parcel means money coming to you.

CAT—A black cat that comes to your house means difficulties caused by treachery. Drive it away and avoid trouble.

CHAIN—If your chain breaks while you are wearing it means disappointments or a broken engagement of marriage.

CLOTHES—To put on clothes the wrong way out is a sign of good luck; but you must not alter them, or the luck will change.

CLOVER—To find a four-leaf clover means luck to you, happiness and prosperity.

COW—Coming in your yard or garden is a very prosperous sign.

CRICKETS—A lucky omen. It predicts money coming to you. Do not disturb them.

DOG—A dog coming to your house means faithful friends and a favorable sign.

DEATH-WATCH—A clicking in the wall by this little insect is regarded as evil, but it does not necessarily mean a death; possibly only some sickness.

EARS—You are being talked about if your ear tingles. Some say, "right for spite, left for love." Others reverse this omen. If you think of the person, friend, or acquaintance who is likely to be talking about you, and mention the name aloud, the tingling will cease if you say the right one.

FLAG—If it falls from the staff while flying it means danger from wounds inflicted by an enemy.

FRUIT STONES OR PITS—Think of a wish first, and then count your stones or pits. If the number is even, the omen is good. If odd, the reverse is the case.

GRASSHOPPER—In the house means some great friend or distinguished person will visit you.

HORSESHOE—To find one means it will bring you luck.

KNIVES—Crossed are a bad omen. If a knife or fork falls to the ground and sticks in the floor you will have a visitor.

LADYBIRDS—Predict visitors.

LOOKING GLASS—To break one means it will bring you bad luck.

MAGPIES—One, bad luck; two, good luck; three, a wedding; four, a birth.

MARRIAGE—A maid should not wear colors; a widow never white. Happy omens for brides are sunshine and a cat sneezing.

MAY—"Marry in May, and you'll rue the day."

NEW MOON—On a Monday signifies good luck and good weather. The new moon seen for the first time over the right shoulder offers the chance for a wish to come true.

NIGHTINGALE—Lucky for lovers if heard before the cuckoo.

OWLS—Are evil omens. Continuous hooting of owls in your trees is said to predict ill-health.

PIGS—To meet a sow coming towards you is good; but if she turns away, the luck flies.

RABBITS—A rabbit running across your path is said to be unlucky.

RAT—A rat running in front of you means treacherous servants and losses through enemies.

RAVEN—To see one, means death to the aged or trouble generally.

SALT—Spilled means a quarrel. This may be avoided by throwing a pinch over the left shoulder.

SCISSORS—If they fall and stick in the floor it means quarrels, illness, separation of lovers.

SERPENT OR SNAKE—If it crosses your path, means bad luck. Kill it and your luck will be reversed.

SHOES—The right shoe is the best one to put on first.

SHOOTING STARS—If you make a wish while the star is still moving, your wish will come true.

SINGING—Before breakfast, you'll cry before night.

SPIDERS—The little red spider is the money spider, and means good fortune coming to you. It must not be disturbed. Long-legged spiders are also forerunners of good fortune.

TOWEL—To wipe your hands on a towel at the same time with another, means you are to quarrel with him or her in the near future.

WHEEL—The wheel coming off any vehicle you are riding in means you are to inherit some fortune, a good omen.

WASHING HANDS—If you wash your hands in the water just used by another, a quarrel may be expected, unless you first make the sign of the cross over the water.

The world is mysterious and mystical and much is still unknown about the nature of time. Is it so hard to believe that we can foretell the future through tea, omens, or another process of divination? If you open your hearts and your minds, you will find a world filled with magic beyond your comprehension. Just put on a pot of hot water, sit back and relax, and get ready to enjoy a lovely cup of tea...and maybe a little secret knowledge of what tomorrow brings.

APPENDIX 1:

Answers to Tea Quizzes

If you'd like to test your knowledge of tea leaf reading, the best thing to do is try a reading on a friend or family member. There's nothing like actual experience to expand your knowledge. Choose your tea, study your symbols and read the leaves! Good luck!

Find the answers to your tea quizzes below:

QUIZ: A HISTORY OF TEA

1. Tea has been a hot beverage, most probably…

a. For 10,000 years old

b. For 5,000 years old

c. Since the Last Supper

d. Since The Boxer Rebellion

e. For 300 years

2. This Chinese emperor, interested in health and the sciences, most likely discovered brewed tea

accidentally when a tea leaf floated into his cup
of hot water:

a. Eisai

b. Bodhidharma

c. Shen Nung

d. Confucius

e. Mao Tse Tung

3. True or False: Tea as a brewed beverage was
mostly likely spread from country to country in
the early years by Trappist Monks.
False, by Buddhist Monks.

4. Brewed tea originally appeared in…

a. England

b. China

c. Persia

d. Japan

e. India

5. True or False: Tea was universally greeted in England with great enthusiasm and all welcomed it into their homes and hearths.

False. Tea caused much controversy in England with many naysayers criticizing the new beverage.

6. _____ is largely credited with starting the British custom of afternoon tea in the early nineteenth century.

a. Lady Grey

b. Queen Victoria

c. Thomas Garraway

d. The Duchess of Bedford

e. Mary Shelly

7. True or False: The English traded one bad habit (opium) for one good habit (tea).

Essentially true. In order to satisfy their unquenchable thirst for tea, the British engaged in opium smuggling and trading with China.

8. The Boston Tea Party was the Colonists reaction
   to...

a. Being forced to drink tea with milk and sugar.

b. A visit from the King.

c. A desire to overthrow tea drinking and replace it
   with coffee.

d. An Mohawk rebellion.

e. Taxation without representation.

QUIZ: THE ABCS OF TEA

1. True or False: Orange Pekoe tea is an herbal tea made with orange peel, assam, and bergomat.
   False. Orange Pekoe is a grade of tea, not a type of tea. See chapter two!

2. The following country leads the world in tea consumption:
   a. England
   b. Ireland
   c. China
   d. Japan
   e. United States

3. Which of the following is not a black tea?
   a. Assam
   b. Darjeeling
   c. Orange Pekoe

d. Ceylon

e. Keemun

4. Which of the following is not a green tea?

a. Sencha

b. Bancha

c. Gunpowder

d. Matcha

e. Chai

5. True or False: All green teas are semi-fermented during manufacture.

False. Both oolongs and black teas are fermented (oolongs are only semi-fermented, but by and large most green teas are not fermented.

6. True or False: Herbal tea comes from the Camellia sinensis plant.

False

7. Which of the following gentlemen was not associated with tea?

a. Thomas Garraway

b. Thomas Lipton

c. Thomas Sullivan

d. Thomas Jefferson

e. Thomas Twining

8. Tea bricks were used for:

a. Money

b. Food

c. Brewing

d. None of the above

e. All of the above

QUIZ: TEA CUSTOMS AROUND THE WORLD

1. True or False. Tea is produced on every continent
   in the world.

   False

2. True or False. African mint tea is always served cold

   False

3. The following is not customarily served at an
   English cream tea;

a. Strawberry jam

b. Scones

c. Milk and sugar

d. Butter

e. Whipped cream

4. Clotted cream is made in:

a. The West Country of England.

b. All over the world.

c. In Australian sheep-herding country.

d. In factories in New York City.

e. On farms in southern France.

5. Which of the following statement is true of the
   Japanese tea ceremony:

a. It is a meditation.

b. There are precise rules and procedures to follow.

c. The ceremony takes place outside in a tea garden.

d. a and b

e. a and c

6. True or False: There is essentially no difference
   between the Japanese and Chinese tea
   ceremonies.

   False

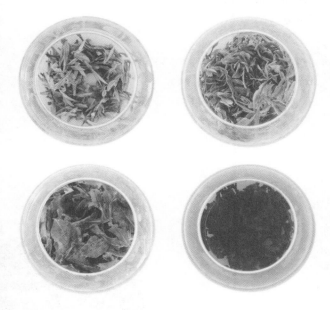

7. True or False. The United States is one of the
   top producers of tea.
   False

8. True or False: Australians by and large prefer to
   teabags to loose leaf tea.
   True

QUIZ: DR. TEA—
TEST YOUR TEA HEALTH KNOWLEDGE

1. The following components of tea make it a
   healthful beverage choice:
a. Polyphenols
b. Tannins
c. Antioxidants
d. flavanoids
e. All of the above

2. True or False: Tea might promote weight loss.
   True

3. True or False: Gargling with green tea might
   prevent an incidence of flu.
   True

4. Tea has been shown to prevent:

a. Hair loss

b. Menstrual cramps

c. Hunger pains

d. Headaches

e. Tooth decay

5. True or False: Drinking large amounts of tea might prevent gastrointestinal distress.
   False

6. Tea might help prevent the onset of the following diseases:

a. Rheumatoid arthritis

b. Prostate cancer

c. Multiple sclerosis

d. a and b

e. b and c

7. True or False: One possible adverse effect of drinking too much tea is insomnia.

True

8. True or False: Green tea is a good substitute for an annual visit to your GP.

False

APPENDIX TWO:

The Chemistry of Tea

The following chapter is taken from the book *Tea Leaves*, written at the turn of the nineteenth century by the merchant Frances Leggett. It contains much interesting information regarding tea.

Chemistry and Physiological Aspects of Tea

If the reader desires an example of imperfect and arrested knowledge in some of the common affairs of life, let him collate the statements of scientific experts concerning the physiological effects upon mankind, of tea. He will then admit that "in a multitude of counselors there is confusion."

Without pretending to more than the rudiments of chemical or physiological science, we shall attempt to examine the nature of tea, and its effects upon the human system; taking as a basis for our remarks Professor Jas. F. Johnston's Chemistry of Common Life, from which work more recent writers draw most of their inspiration.

Chemists find in manufacturing tea leaves three principal constituents to which all the physiological effects of tea are attributed. These are, (1) Theine, (2) Essential or Volatile Oils, (3) Tannin.

Theine is present in the green leaf of tea, and is apparently unchanged in the manufactured leaf and in the infusion or beverage. We regard it as the one essential and the most valuable element of all teas, physiologically considered. Strangely enough, theine is the one important constituent which is entirely neglected by the tea-tester and the trader. In testing and grading teas for purchase and sale, their appearance, odor and taste, their color and body when "drawn," determine their pecuniary value, without relation to their percentage of theine, or its effects upon the tester.

Theine has been found in nature in but a few plants, as in tea, in coffee, (then termed caffeine), in Mat'e (Paraguay or Brazilian tea), and in the Kola nut of Africa. A very similar principle, having analogous properties, but containing more nitrogen, exists in cocoa, (theobroma).

Theine, when isolated by heat from the tea leaf or infusions, condenses in minute white needles or crystals, having no odor and but a faintly bitter taste. In manufactured tea leaves, theine constitutes from one to five percent of their weight. According to Professor Johnston, three or four grains per day of this substance may be taken without injury by most persons; or such quantity as would be contained in half and ounce of Chinese black tea. Indian (Assam) tea and Ceylon tea, being stronger in theine, would suffice in lesser quantity.

Theine is soluble in about 100 parts of hot water. It vaporizes at 185 degrees Celsius or 365 degrees Fahrenheit, hence it is not driven off by continued boiling of tea infusion.

W. Dittmar found by experiment that prolonged steeping of tea leaves up to ten minutes increased the proportion of theine in the infusion. His results are:

STEEPED 5 MINUTES

Average of 8 samples Chinese tea:

Theine, percent infusion—2.58

Tannin—3.06

Average of 6 samples Ceylon tea:

Theine—3.15

Tannin—5.87

Average of 12 samples of Indian tea:

Theine—3.63

Tannin—6.77

STEEPED 10 MINUTES

Average of 8 samples of Chinese tea:

Theine—2.79—Increase about 10 percent

Tannin—3.78—Increase about 25 percent

Average of 6 samples Ceylon tea:

Theine—3.29—Increase about 5 percent

Tannin—7.30—Increase about 25 percent

Average of 12 samples of Indian tea:

Theine—3.73—Increase about 3 percent

Tannin—8.09—Increase about 20 percent

W. M. Green reported that in prolonging the steeping of tea from 10 to 20 minutes, he observed the formation of a tannate of theine, which diminished the proportion of 1.30 percent of theine at 10 minutes to 1.16 percent after 20 minutes steeping, a loss of about 10 percent, unless the latter salt so formed is proved to yield up its theine constituent in the human stomach.

While theine is credited as the source of the most powerful and useful properties of tea, and without which no plant would be recognized as tea, yet some of the stimulating or exhilarating influences of this plant are attributed to the volatile oils which contribute so largely to the flavors and odors which characterize tea.

These Essential or Volatile Oils of manufactured tea are said to reside in the minute cells of the green leaf, but they are greatly changed by manipulation, for they are not manifest to the sense of taste or smell when expressed from the green leaf by bruising, nor does the green leaf yield their aromatic flavors to an infusion. Professor Johnston says that these precious oils are artificially developed by manufacture. David Crole declares that they are developed "to a certain extent during withering, and also during the first stage of firing," which last process, if carelessly conducted, "oxidizes it (the oil) into resin."

Green tea, they first remove from the green leaf, imparts very little flavor or scent to its infusion. In some Oolong Black teas, and in some Ceylon Black teas, these oils are highly developed and are very fragrant. In the black Souchongs and Congous they have again been altered by treatment, but are no less perceptible, and to many, are quite as agreeable. Although constituting only one-half to one percent by weight of the dried leaf, these oils are all-important to the trademan and to the consumer.

These volatile oils are strongest in new teas, and are gradually wasted by exposure to the atmosphere. Robert Fortune and other travelers in China have stated that the Chinese will not use new teas, but allow them to pass through a sort of "ripening" process. Mr. Crole, speaking probably of the Indian teas with which he was so familiar as a planter and chemist, says that "tea should always be kept for a year before being drank. If the infusion of freshly manufactured tea is drank, it causes violent diarrhea; therefore it should be kept a year before it is consumed, in order to let it mellow."

There is no doubt that the more impervious the package containing tea is to the air, the more perfectly the finer qualities of the tea are preserved. If there is a necessity for ripening or mellowing by time, air should be rigidly excluded during that period.

As to the keeping qualities of fine teas, in tight packages, we know that they are not spoiled or injured by two years storage in this climate.

Tannin is the third important element of the tea leaf, and it varies greatly in percentage in different teas, and increases with the age of the growing leaf. It is the cause of the rasping, puckering, astringent effect upon the tongue and interior of the mouth.

Tannin in tea has been a great bugbear with the ill-informed, bit it is not nearly so deleterious as some careless or unscrupulous writers would have us believe. In the first place there is a very insignificant quantity of tannin in properly drawn teas, say in those drawn for not longer than five or eight minutes. The tannin present in a fine Black tea, steeped at a moderate temperature for fifteen or twenty minutes will not harm a delicate stomach. We take quite as much tannin in some fruits, and make no fuss about it. Secondly, if a strong solution of tannin is taken into the stomach and there comes in contact with albuminous or gelatinous foods, it will expend its coagulating power upon such substances. If there are no such substances present, it is the expressed opinion of Mr. Crole (in a discussion upon the chemistry of tea) that the tannin is converted into glucose and other harmless products by the digestive processes. The wild declarations that tea tannin "tans" the coating of the stomach into a leathery condition is without foundation. Even where too prolonged steeping has greatly increased the usual proportion of tannin in tea infusion, milk, when added, neutralizes the coagulating power of the tannin entirely or to such degree as to render it harmless.

Professor Johnston thinks it quite probable that tannin takes some part in the exhilarating effect of tea, and in that of the betel-nut of the East. While the astringent influence of strong tannin upon the bowels is regarded as unfavorable, hot tea infusion has with many persons a contrary effect, stimulating the peristaltic movements and antagonizing constipation.

If tannin is injurious, it should be observed that its

proportion in the leaf of green teas is very much larger than in Black teas. An analysis by Mulder gave as the percentage of tannin in a Black tea, 12.85 percent, and in a green tea as 17.80 percent. But another analysis made by Y. Kazai, of the Imperial College of Agriculture of Japan, made the percentage of tannin (gallo-tannic acid) in a Green tea 10.64, and in a Black tea from the same leaf 4.89. In the green leaf from which these teas were derived he found 12.91 percent of tannin. This analysis indicates also that a portion of the tannin disappears in manufacturing Green tea, but a still larger proportion is lost or changed in the manufacture of Black tea.

Tannic acid taken into the human stomach in large quantity produces, according to the U.S. Dispensatory, "only a mild gastro-intestinal irritation."

Passing over the phosphoric acid, the gluten, and other interesting constituents of the tea leaf, we proceed to the observed effects of tea upon the human system.

Professor Johnston (before quoted) says that tea "exhilarates without sensibly intoxicating. It excites the brain to increased activity and produces wakefulness; hence its usefulness to hard students, to those who have vigils to keep, and to persons who labor much with the head. It soothes, on the contrary, and stills the vascular system, (arteries, veins, capillaries, etc.), and hence its use in inflammatory diseases, and as a cure for headaches. Green tea, when strong, acts very powerfully on some constitutions, producing nervous tremblings and other distressing symptoms, acting as a narcotic, and in inferior animals even producing paralysis. Its exciting effect upon the nerves makes it useful in counteracting the effects of fermented liquors, and the stupor sometimes induced by fever." And again, tea "lessens waste," and diminishes the quantity of food required; "saves food; stands to a certain extent in the place of food, while at the same time it soothes the body and enlivens the mind."

Professor A. H. Church, of Oxon, England, in one of his often quoted books on Food, says that "the infusion of tea has little nutritive value, but it increases respiratory action, and excites the brain to greater activity."

J.C. Hutchinson, M.D., (late President Medical Society of State of New York), remarks that caffeine, which he regards as identical with theine, "is a gentle stimulant, without any injurious reaction. It produces a restful feeling after exhausting efforts of mind or body; it tranquilizes but does not disqualify for labor, and therefore it is highly esteemed by persons of literary pursuits. The excessive use of either tea or coffee will cause wakefulness."

Dr. Kane, the Artic Explorer, speaking of the diet of his men while sojourning in the Artic ice fields, said that his men preferred coffee in the mornings, but at night, "tea soothed them after a hard day's labor, and better enabled them to sleep."

Dr. Edward Smith, an English Physiologist, in an

address before the Royal Medical and Chirurgical Society, remarked that "tea increased waste in the body, excited every function, and was well fitted to cases where there was a superfluity of material in the system;—but is injurious to the under-fed, or where there is greater waste than supply." Dr. Smith recommended tea as a preventive of heat apoplexy, and in cases of suspended animation, as from partial drowning.

We have selected these expressions of opinion from among a large number of diverse character, for the purpose of illustrating the uncertainty of knowledge concerning tea. To recapitulate: Professor Johnston finds that tea exhilarates; excites to activity, produces wakefulness; yet it sooths, and it tranquilizes the vascular system; it lessens waste and saves food.

Dr. Smith found tea to increase waste, and to be injurious where food is deficient; says tea excites every function,—which must include the vascular system.

Dr. Hutchinson and Dr. Kane agree in the main.

What is the meaning of such radical differences of view? First, tea affects different persons very differently; secondly, the subject has not received that careful study which it merits, and thirdly, there is a careless confounding of at least three classes of effects, and a confusion of terms in describing them.

We feel an unaffected diffidence in criticizing and endeavoring to improve upon the expressions of scientific men of honest purpose, but we may be pardoned for pointing the way to a more careful analysis of the merits and deficiencies of an article of diet used by so many millions of people.

We find among the ordinary effects of tea-drinking:

Exhilaration—an elevation of feeling, a lightness of mood or spirits; a cheerfulness or even joy, which is compatible with rest. This effect may be entirely independent of pure stimulus, or of any disposition to mental or physical activity.

• Stimulation—a quickening or rousing to action of

any faculty, but as usually employed, an urging to action of bodily or mental powers.

• Sustaining—enabling one to continue the expenditure of energy with less sense of fatigue, at the time, or afterwards.

• Refreshing—relieving or reviving after exertion of any kind; reanimating, invigorating; contributing to rest after fatigue.

• Exciting—in the sense of stimulation of brain and nervous system to higher tension, but not necessarily attended by disposition to labor or useful activity.

Now some tea-drinkers find in the beverage exhilaration only, a lightness of mood, but they are disposed to rest and to reverie, to simply a passive meditation, or an indulgence of the imagination.

Others are stimulated to mental or to physical activity, and are sustained during such action. Afterwards they are refreshed when fatigued, by the same beverage.

Others again are nervously excited and cannot rest or

sleep; but are too "nervous," as they express it, to set about any formal task, especially of a mental character.

We have known tea-drinkers, too, who after a hard day's toil, could drink two or three cups of strong tea and lie down to sleep for the night as quietly as babes are expected to—but do not.

It must be evident that each person should observe the effects of tea upon himself or herself and be governed accordingly. Tea is poison to some temperaments, and so are strawberries. Tea will cure a headache or may produce one; will dispose to rest or excite to action. We will sum then by conceding that all our quoted authorities are right in their conclusions, if limited to a limited class of tea-drinkers, and all are wrong, in a very broad application.

Theine is the one constant agency in the effects of tea. It is present in teas that are devoid of essential oils—so far as the senses go—and it still refreshes, stimulates, sustains, and exhilarates.

The feeling of "comfort," attributed by some writers to the hot water of the tea, may be also enjoyed by drinking cold tea, which is no less refreshing in hot weather. The high-flavored essential oils (strictly oils which evaporate at very moderate temperatures) of Formosa teas seem to take part in the superior exhilarating or almost intoxicating effects of the choice varieties, but we have no certain proof of the fact; while the more intoxicating and stimulating, as well as deleterious, green teas possess very little, if any, of these pleasant oils.

It seems to be an orthodox opinion among physiologists that tea contributes nothing toward support of the human system; that it only rouses it into action, an effect which should, consistently, be followed by corresponding reaction and depression, which plainly is not the case. This hypothesis leaves the enquiring layman in a dilemma. Tea must either enable the system to draw more heavily or more economically upon the

resources afforded by recognized food, or it is itself
nutriment. Otherwise, an established principle of
physics—that there can be no expenditure of energy
without correlative cost—would be subverted. As tea is
admitted upon experience to be most useful, and most
craved by mankind, where the supply of food is insufficient; and as it is known to refresh and sustain in large
degree in the absence of any food whatever, there is fair
ground for the opinion, however heterodox, that tea
directly affords nutriment to the human organism, and,
possibly, to the brain and nerves in particular, as with
phosphoric acid.

Animal gelatine has been placed in the same class
with tea by Liebig, Dr. John W. Draper, and others, and
it is asserted that it conserves waste without itself
entering into the substance of human tissue. It is an
accepted physiological law that nothing taken as food
or drink can support expenditure of human energy in
sensible motion, in heat, or in the nervous waste of

mental or emotional exercise without first being built up into living tissue; the breaking down or chemical decomposition of which tissue, and subsequent oxidation of less complex compounds or their constituents, is the direct source of bodily energy of every description. This, at least, is our reading of modern authorities, like Foster. If tea and gelatine, and possibly alcohol, are to form exceptions to the law, the law no longer stands. But it would seem more reasonable to amend the hypothesis concerning exceptions, and bring them into line by admitting that they are nutritious in a manner not yet ascertained. All physiological laws are provisional, good until proved insufficient, and then to be amended in the light of accumulating facts.

Resources

BOOKS AND MAGAZINES

A Highland Seer, *Tea-Cup Reading, and the Art of Fortune Telling by Tea Leaves*, public domain.

Francis Leggett & Company, *Tea Leaves*, 1900, public domain.

Kakuzo, Okakura, *The Book of Tea*, public domain.

Kent, Cicely, *Telling Fortunes By Tea Leaves: How to Read Your Fate in a Teacup*, 1922, public domain.

Perry, Sarah, *The New Tea Book*. Chronicle Books, San Francisco, CA, 2001.

Pettigrew, Jane, *The Tea Companion*. Running Press, Philadelphia, PA, 2004.

Rasmussen, Wendy, and Rhinehart, Rick, *Tea Basics*. John Wiley and Sons, Hoboken, NJ, 1999.

Rubin, Ron, and Gold, Stuart Avery, *Tea Chings: The Tea and Herb Companion*. Newmarket Press, NY, NY, 2002.

WEBSITES

Africa Tea
http://www.africatea.com, www.africatea.com

ANTIQUE BOXES at the Sign of the Hygra
http://www.users.globalnet.co.uk/~boxes/
boxweb/teacaddy.htm

The Association of Small Collector of Antique Silver
http://www.ascasonline.org/articolowastebowl.html

Australian Food and Drug Council
http://www.tea.org.au

CBS News
http://www.cbsnews.com/stories/2006/11/29/the_skin-
ny/main2213840.shtml

Dilmah
www.dilmahtea.com

FML Tea
http://www.fmltea.com/health/9.htm

The Fragrant Leaf
www.thefragantleaf.com

Marvel Creations
www.marvelcreations.com

Numi Tea
http://www.worldpantry.com/cgi-bin/ncommerce3/
ExecMacro/numitea/store.d2w/report

Planet Tea
www.planet-tea.com

The Republic of Tea
www.republicoftea.com

Stash Tea

http://www.stashtea.com/

Tea Lovers.com

http://greentealovers.com/greenteahealthcancer.htm

Tea USA.org

http://www.teausa.org/general/teasym/400fc.cfm

Teavana

http://www.teavana.com/

Upton Tea

http://www.uptontea.com/shopcart/information/
INFOcustoms.asp

Index